Creating Small Church Communities

A Plan for Restructuring the Parish and Renewing Parish Life

(Third Edition)

Arthur R. Baranowski

ST. ANTHONY MESSENGER PRESS

Cincinnati, Ohio

Nihil Obstat: Rev. Donald Miller, O.F.M.
                     Rev. Robert J. Buschmiller
Imprimi Potest: Rev. John Bok, O.F.M.
                     Provincial
Imprimatur: +Most Rev. Carl K. Moeddel, V.G.
                     Archdiocese of Cincinnati
                     October 3, 1996

The *nihil obstat* and *imprimatur* are a declaration that a book is considered to be free from doctrinal or moral error. It is not implied that those who have granted the *nihil obstat* and *imprimatur* agree with the contents, opinions or statements expressed.

Scripture citations are taken from the *New Revised Standard Version Bible,* © 1989 by the Division of Christian Education of the National Council of the Churches of Christ in the U.S.A. and used by permission.

Cover design by Julie Lonneman
Book design by Mary Alfieri
Electronic format and pagination by Sandra Digman

ISBN 0-86716-275-9

Published by St. Anthony Messenger Press
www.AmericanCatholic.org

Printed in the U.S.A.

*To the pastors, administrators and parish leaders
structuring parishes to ensure that
the ordinary people help each other
connect everyday life and faith regularly*

CONTENTS

ACKNOWLEDGMENTS

To Kathleen O'Reilly and Carrie Piro, my collaborators. This pastoral plan and the support materials which accompany it are possible only because of them. Together we formed a pastoral staff and shared the vision and the work.

To Lawrence and Judy Berch; the Reverends Tim Babcock, David Harvey and C. Richard Kelly; and Raymond Maloney. These readers of my first draft contributed to the clarity, depth and zest of this book.

To Father Tim Babcock and the staff of St. Mary's Parish, Royal Oak, Michigan, for providing me with a home while I was writing.

To Jim and Linda Pipp for having the first draft typed at their own expense.

To Jean Suzor for typing the revision.

To all those who have given me the experience of being part of the church.

May the Lord reward them all!

FOREWORD

This book is written to promote the restructuring of parishes in two equally important and necessary ways. The first restructuring involves the existing parish programs, committees, and organizations. Everything that happens in the parish would include some time for a life reflection question (sometimes, more than one question is used), a little quiet, and a listening to each other in small groups of two or three, if possible. This structure for the existing parish activities is done sensitively and appropriately to each particular program/committee and to the people involved.

The second restructuring of parish and what this book speaks to primarily is the restructuring of parishes into small church communities. I believe that our deliberate pastoral plan to bring parishioners together in small groups of eight to 12 adults at St. Elizabeth Seton Parish in Troy, Michigan, can serve as a model for any parish, for all parishes. This book is an effort to share the vision which inspired us as well as the nuts and bolts of how we did what we did.

I have also included actual testimonies—stories—from a variety of parishioners about how this restructuring touched their lives and called them to be church. For the small church communities which we created in our restructuring *did become church* at this most basic level. They slowly evolved to include formation, prayer and service, the activities of the church at the parish level.

All parishes already have some small communities within them. But our vision foresees all parishioners experiencing their Catholic identity in these smaller, church communities, and our plan helps a parish work gradually and persistently toward that goal—even though the goal is never fully achieved.

We came to use the term *Small Church Communities (SCCs)* to name these little churches within the parish. For some this will call to mind the *communidades de base* of Latin America. The vision of the Latin American experience is the same: to create a parish where the ordinary people help each other connect everyday life and faith. But, the tactics or the ways of achieving that kind of parish will differ because the culture is different and the style of parish is different. And *parish* is the continuing frame of reference for the small church communities we speak about in this book.

"Called to Be Church," the step-by-step process for moving a parish toward total restructuring into small communities, enhances and supports parish. It grows out of one particular parish's experience (St. Elizabeth Seton's) and from my own 28 years of working with several parishes as they restructured into small communities. Yet this parish plan transcends me and my experience.

I am an ordinary parish priest—hardworking, but ordinary. Any parish can do what we did at St. Elizabeth Seton. Parishes throughout the United States, Canada and Australia are restructuring into small church communities. These parishes have formed a national association, the National Alliance for Parishes Restructuring into Communities (NAPRC, 1000 Michigan Ave., Marysville, MI 48040-1466, 810-364-3500).

Small Church Communities work! Ordinary Catholic people can *become* the church rather than go *to* church. Most significantly, through SCCs parishioners experience that they do make an appreciable difference for others in the church. They realize they have a human and spiritual contribution to give—instead of simply receiving truth or inspiration from the programs offered by the parish. Their lives are never the same again. Neither is the life of the parish.

This book is intended for any Catholic, of any age, who wants to take a first step in renewing his or her own parish. That first step can be as simple as sharing this book with the pastor or parish staff or with a few fellow parishioners. The reflection questions throughout are meant to encourage sharing with a few others and to help a small group put the theory of this book into practice.

Why Change Your Parish?

*I*n the 25 years since Vatican II, Catholic parishes have tried a great number of programs to renew the church and to renew individual parishioners. Many of these programs are very creative. Yet the one renewal process that has not been attempted is to change the parish structure itself. And this is precisely, I believe, the primary renewal need today.

Why Restructure?

Parishes need to restructure because parishes, as we now have them, are ineffective. There are exceptions, of course, but they remain exceptions. And this shouldn't be surprising. Our present world is different enough from even the recent past to demand a different structure for bringing Catholics together in the parish.

American Catholics today move more often than a generation ago, have less stable relationships, experience less control over their lives and their families' lives and, in the midst of it all, have the "good life" and the "real thing" preached to them daily by a consumer society. The individual often counts for little and feels isolated and alone. In a technological world, it is very easy to live day by day, staying on the surface of experience, never questioning the basic assumptions of society.

Yet the life-style asked of the disciple by Christ and by the church involves a conversion of life based on daily reflection. This life-style demands decisions that are definitely countercultural. Will such a life-style emerge when most Catholics only experience church for one hour each week in a formal setting?

In addition to the problem of culture, some present parish trends themselves make the church less effective in people's lives. The North American parish, for example, is no longer the center for Catholic family life, education and recreation. And the transiency of modern people has an enormous effect on a parish because a large part of the parish's population will change in just a few years. The fact is, today's urban or suburban parish no longer has 50 years of stable neighborhood life as a base on which to build slowly a sense of community and a value system around Jesus Christ.

Another continuing trend is toward large parishes where staff people specialize in education, worship or outreach—and this specialization can easily become compartmentalization. As a result, parishes can have many activities without having a specific, clear-cut and workable plan for bringing people together to reinforce each other as Catholic Christians struggling to live a gospel life-style. Rather than adding more programs and activities in an attempt to reach people, the time is here to look at the way the parish brings its people together in the first place. Is the present parish structure effective for what a parish is meant to do?

The Why of a Parish

Underneath all the activities and statements of mission or purpose, the parish is meant to foster two basic realities: an experience of *love* and an experience of *faith*. And the very first of these should be love.

An ordinary sense of care and responsibility for each other should pervade a parish. The bottom line that keeps a family together through many crises and disagreements is that members understand they are loved and they, in turn, love the others in the family. That is the bottom line for church, too. Whatever else a Catholic knows, he or she must absolutely

2

know that he or she is valued by the people of the church. Christ himself cites love as a top priority for the church community: "This is how all will know you for my disciples: your love for one another" (John 13:35).

Love has to be specific. I have to be known *as a person.* Love is much more than the warm feeling at the Sunday liturgy where everyone may feel close for a while or the friendliness at the coffee-and-donut social afterwards. The liturgy may be moving and participatory. Yet, is a Catholic noticed and cared for simply by belonging to the church?

Many parishes care very much for their sick, homeless and broken. Catholics do respond generously to the downtrodden and to causes brought to their attention. Nevertheless, many people get lost "between the cracks" in most parishes, especially if the parish staff doesn't note the needs people have.

Parishioners themselves don't notice each other all that well in most parishes, except for involved people or people in critical situations. We don't manifest ordinary, everyday care for each other because parishes are not structured to help us get to know each other. We preach caring in our programs, our religious education and our homilies; but our parishes don't bring people together in a way that they can easily care about each other.

Is your parish known for the care parishioners have for each other?

Do most Catholics even expect to be loved in their parish? Do you? How would various individuals in your parish respond to these questions: Am I known? Is anyone praying for me? Is anyone responsible for me? How would you answer?

The second basic a parish should provide is an experience of faith. God or Jesus becomes more real for us when we share our faith—or lack of faith—with one another because sharing helps us notice God and take the Lord seriously. Somehow God has to be found in our everyday life. Ordinary Catholics—

working people, office professionals, young adults, seniors—have faith, but often they don't trust the faith that is in them. Most Catholics need help from others who care about them and know a little about their journey of faith before they learn to trust their own experiences.

Does the life experience of ordinary parishioners ever get a hearing in your parish? Does your experience of life?

Does the ordinary Catholic in your parish know that the church is poorer for not having heard his or her experience of life? Do you?

Specific parish groups, like prayer groups or Scripture classes, may share faith in a personal way, but does the entire community? Certain motivated people, like catechists, may reflect together on their faith journeys, but is the entire parish a people listening to each other and reflecting on how God is found in their life?

The way we come together as church is primary. That is what teaches us—not simply our programs. Faith and love are experiences. The more these experiences are shared—and this can happen best in a small group—the more people notice God and God's call to be church for one another.

The parish as presently structured no longer brings us together to experience well what makes us Catholic Christians. The new Rite of Christian Initiation of Adults, in contrast, provides the model of what the parish community is meant to be.

Does your parish help members know others and become known specifically enough to care and be cared for?

Does your parish help members listen to each other so they learn to trust their own experiences of God and discern God's call in their lives?

RCIA—A Model for Being Catholic

The Rite of Christian Initiation of Adults (RCIA) is the process for incorporating adult inquirers into the church. But the RCIA is much more than an initiation process for that small group that enters the church at the Easter Vigil. It provides a mirror for seeing clearly who we are as the church. For the way we bring newcomers into the church says a great deal about what being the church means to the rest of us.

The heart of RCIA is the Catechumenate. It creates a small-group setting where trust can build; invites participants to get in touch with their own faith stories ("How has God been active in my life and how have I responded over the years?"); encourages participants to share their faith stories with each other, challenges participants to compare their personal faith stories to that of the church; provides an experience of the care, interest, prayer and support from the people of the church during the RCIA journey.

Each person's pace is respected; no one is ever rushed. The formation is not only intellectual (learning the beliefs of Catholics), but the formation involves the total person's history and experience and also involves personal warm, sharing relationships with a few members of the church. The community's story in Scripture and Tradition gives a focus of meaning to the individual's experience. In other words, this new rite, now mandated by the U.S. bishops as the way all parishes are to welcome new members into the church, gets back to the basics of *becoming* a Catholic Christian and *being* a Catholic Christian. Just as the Catechumenate calls participants to an ongoing, experiential process involving the total person and bonding the person to others in the community through mutual prayer and faith-sharing, so are all the rest of us called to that process by the very fact that we are church.

But is this how we see ourselves as church, experience ourselves as church? Is the wider parish the kind of church the RCIA prepares catechumens to be initiated into?

Does your parish create small-group settings where parishioners can learn to trust one another?

Does your parish invite parishioners to get in touch with their own faith stories and encourage sharing with others?

Does your parish challenge individuals to compare their faith stories to the church's story in Scripture and Tradition? Does your parish provide an ongoing experience of care, interest, prayer and support for each parishioner?

The RCIA presents a vision for the whole church. It was intended to be a renewal process for the entire parish as well as for the newcomer to the church. But how can this RCIA-inspired renewal proceed?

I don't see how the ordinary Catholic in the average parish can be Catholic in the way modeled in the RCIA without a smaller, more personal experience of church than is accessible in most parishes today. I also don't see how we are going to keep our promise of church to the catechumens entering through the RCIA process without making some smaller experience of church available. Many catechumenate leaders already report how easily newcomers get lost in the big parish after the Easter Vigil. The RCIA process touched them significantly. But now these new Catholics have no real support group to help them keep growing in faith and love. Most parishes simply do not have an ongoing means to help Catholics reflect on the events of their lives, connect these with the church's story and, from there, make some kind of life commitment.

What can be done about this? Some places react by figuring out a better RCIA program that will just continue longer after Easter. But we don't need a better program; we need a better church. We need a church that is itself a more obvious experience of sharing faith and caring for each other. How can we get this "better church"? By restructuring the parish into smaller churches, into Small Church Communities. Not prayer groups, not Scripture study groups, not another program of any kind—but permanent or semi-permanent Small Church Communities. And we need to structure the present parish activities to allow parishioners in those activities to connect life and faith with each other, even if only for a few minutes at a time.

I hope this book can be one step toward that better Church.

Does your parish enable you to keep growing as a Catholic?

Does it bring you together with others for prayer and connecting of everyday life and faith in a regular, ongoing way?

When the RCIA is held up as a mirror to your parish, what does it reveal? Does the way you incorporate new members into the church reveal the way you really are as a church?

A STORY

We are a couple 60 years of age—cradle Catholics, Irish, very traditional. We attended Catholic schools at all levels and made sure our own children did the same.

Both of us did all the Catholic things as we were taught them. We are loyal Catholics, always supported the church financially, and ran the bingo for years at Bishop Foley High School. But we also sat in the back of the church, never touched the host, and went to communion only to the priest. We had faith but it was kept inside. The difference the SCC has made for us personally is to bring us to a different concept of faith.

We no longer *have* to go to church. We *want* to go and share a meal with our parish family.

In the past our faith was a very private matter. Now, however, we can openly discuss our doubts, fears, happiness with those in our group, and know they will help us. We are considerably older than the other members of the group but that doesn't make a difference. The honest sharing—not agreement, but sharing—has helped us to be aware of God in different ways in our own lives.

Because of many job transfers, we have been in many parishes in several states. St. Elizabeth Seton is unique, however. The love and concern shown among the people has to be the result of our small communities. Retirement could come this year for Matt. This is more home to us now than St. Louis, our hometown where we have relatives and old friends. We will probably stay here, if our health holds out, because of these people in our small group and in our parish. We would never have said that a few years ago.

Being Who We Are Better

In many ways the Second Vatican Council got us back to basics by underscoring who we are as church: The church is the whole people of God. Baptism and Confirmation really do give each one of us the calling and the power to be holy, to be responsible for the church's inner life and to take responsibility for the mission of the church in the world.

The great unfinished task of the Council, however, is how to translate this vision into the ordinary Catholic parishioner's daily consciousness and life, how to make the church "we" instead of "they"—and every day, not only Sunday.

Do you see your fellow parishioners, by and large, aware of their calling to be church? Is this an important part of your awareness?

How is your parish making an impact on members' everyday thinking and decision-making? On your everyday thinking and decision-making?

If you are satisfied that your parish at present adequately touches parishioners' daily lives, fine. This plan for restructuring is probably not for you. If, on the other hand, you judge that many people lack awareness of their basic identity as baptized Christians called to be church for one another and for the world, then this new way of being parish can help you and others grow in this identity.

The plan developed at St. Elizabeth Seton for restructuring into smaller faith communities, smaller churches (what we finally came to call Small Church Communities—SCCs) allowed us to affirm this sense of our identity as church. In the process we discovered that what we were really doing was dusting off and polishing up the treasure we always had as the Catholic Christian community. Only now, restructuring was making the treasure available to a much larger number of ordinary parishioners. Small Church Communities helped all of us "be who we are better."

The first step in becoming better at being church is not taking a course or reading the right book. The first step is focusing on the basic process of Christian life, beginning it yourself if you have not already done so, and promoting it among other parishioners. What is this basic process? Discerning God's personal daily call in your life. To discern means to take note of daily events, decisions, personal encounters—and of their effect on you—in order to discover their meaning. Sometimes discernment requires a look back over longer periods of time. Anyone, regardless of education or temperament, can develop discernment skills, but it takes practice and time.

Talking with others who also try to find God in their daily lives helps a great deal; it is, in fact, almost indispensable. Most people in the church at this point in time have nobody to listen to them try to sort out how God might be speaking in their lives. Every baptized person has the right to tell his or her faith story and to get a hearing in the faith community. Without this telling—and the community's response—our consciousness and appreciation of the Lord in our lives develop poorly.

People talk *about* religion easily enough. We can discuss the changes in the church, what we like and dislike in our parish, even a particular theologian or philosophy of life. But most of us find sharing personal faith—what religion *means* to us—more difficult.

More difficult still is taking the next step—comparing my personal experience to the church's experience of the Lord in Scripture, Sacrament and Tradition. Only through making these connections can we discover the Lord who gives a focus to our personal life story through the church's story. This kind of sharing of faith in order to grow more aware of God's presence and action in our lives is essential in living out a Catholic Christian identity in today's world. Being a Catholic Christian has to make a difference experientially, not just theoretically.

But this kind of discernment and sharing of faith usually do not happen in the typical parish for any significant percentage of parishioners for several reasons: First, there is no ongoing means for promoting this kind of discernment and sharing as an essential part of parish life. Second, given the unreflective nature of the world we live in, this kind of discernment and sharing actually demands a counter-cultural way of life that can best be maintained with group support. And the size of most parishes means that the parish as parish is too large a group to provide this support effectively.

Looking to Our Past

This emphasis on the importance of small-group support for living a Catholic life is really nothing new. Even in the most traditional and the largest of parishes at present, small groups of Catholics already meet together regularly and share their lives and their faith at some level. And they always have! All kinds of longstanding small-group associations (parish guilds, the St. Vincent de Paul Society and CFM) as well as newcomers like post-Marriage Encounter groups and RENEW groups and Wednesday morning prayer groups make a big difference for the parish. It's hard to imagine any parish without parishioners relating at some smaller group level. What's different in our vision? We imagine the ideal of *all* parishioners relating that way as the normal course of parish life!

In fact, until the last few centuries, most Catholics did live and relate in relatively small parish communities. Large metropolitan centers where huge numbers of people gather in correspondingly large, impersonal parishes, are a relatively recent phenomenon. Our typical experience of parish today reflects the changing living patterns of modern people. We adapted to large cities and sprawling suburbs. We accommodated the influx of Catholic immigrants that doubled and finally multiplied many times over the number of Catholics in the United States. Still, the usual pattern—the way we did it most of the time over our long history as church—was to relate in small familial parishes. Therefore the large institutional parish of today is the exception rather than the historical rule.

So wanting to restructure the present parish into smaller units is not really a departure from our tradition but a return to it. Our goal is the same "old" Catholic Church where the presence and power of the Holy Spirit will continue to operate—but in a way most effective in our time and place. There is already very real personal faith in the people of the church. Many do pray daily, making decisions based on faith; many are already generous toward the poor and seek ways to change unjust social structures. We only hope to provide a method for Catholics to strengthen in each other their best qualities. The church community is worth our best efforts and loyalty.

This book is written with that assumption. Restructuring allows the parish to become more clearly and experientially the church. Small communities are a practical approach to enhance the faith and genuine love already there—helping us *be who we are better.*

What qualities do you see in the people of the church that help you have confidence in the parish? Name specific people and specific instances.

Is there a way you can find time with one or a few of them to talk about your faith? This book? Your parish?

A STORY

My name is Max. My family and I came to the United States from the United Kingdom 10 years ago because of a job transfer. I am a design engineer by profession.

During my upbringing, experience of organized religion was rather minimal. I had received a bit of instruction in the Anglican Church and had been to services in that church on occasion and the Catholic Church less often. My parents kept their distance from any church and church never seemed to make any difference for life. I would characterize myself as mildly cynical about systems of religion and I never really knew anyone for whom any of it made much difference.

My perception of Sunday services was that the priest was "up there doing his own thing" with no connection to the real life of anybody there. I know now that my past perceptions were biased and those of a distanced observer, but I still find many regular Catholics who admit to coming and going from Mass with little perception of its having any effect on their lives.

My experience of the liturgy at St. Elizabeth Seton was different for several reasons. I was different—a little less critical (but only a little) as I matured. I also had some contact with Catholic neighbors over the years who were positive toward the church and toward life, and my son became interested in the church.

I was baptized into the Catholic community last Easter. Much more happened over the last two years to get me here but the experience of the people at liturgy has had a permanent effect on me. We all belonged and were part of it. The warming toward the church was quite gradual but that warming grew because of how I experienced all of us at Mass. Since then, I have heard other visitors describe our parish with the two qualities that I found there but could not find the words for: reverence for God and care for each other. There is a reverence for God and for each other. You can feel them. I know now that these qualities are more evident at St. Elizabeth Seton through the small communities that keep reinforcing and deepening those qualities.

CHAPTER ONE

A New Way to Be Church

T he vision presented in this book is not unique because it promotes small groups. The church has always known that Catholics meeting in small groups can significantly support each other's faith and the faith of the larger community. Small-group experiences are already renewing the church all over the world.

Nor is this vision just another—albeit "better"—program for Small Church Communities. Excellent programs already exist, and another program is not needed. RENEW is probably the most successful and widespread English language format for small faith-sharing groups in parishes. Other formats also are quite effective for specific groups: Marriage Encounter and Cursillo follow-up meetings, various Scripture-sharing programs and households of charismatic Christians.

What is unique in the small groups we talk about is that they do not remain mere small groups. They become church at a new, more basic level. And the pastoral plan for moving your parish in this direction is not just another program that the parish embraces this year. It changes the very way parishioners come together to be church for each other and for the world and, in the process, radically changes—restructures—the parish forever.

Levels of Belonging

The accompanying diagram shows how the base church—the Small Church Community—fits into the other expressions of church. Each circle represents an expression of church community. The large outside circle is the world-wide community of Catholics, 950 million strong, with the Pope as its pastor. Each inner circle becomes smaller and more experiential.

The large universal church is a communion of dioceses. But each diocese is also a church and is, in fact, a communion of parishes. We are adding still another expression of church: the base church, the Small Church Community. Thus the parish becomes a communion of small communities.

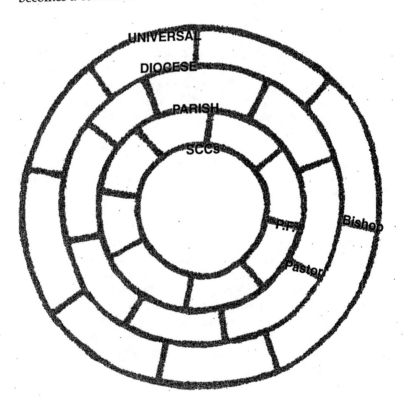

Notice that the link—or the connector—between each expression of the church is the pastoral person: the diocese's bishop, the parish's pastor or administrator and the SCC's pastoral facilitator. The Catholic Church, in fact, exists at many levels. It can be seen as a *communion* of different levels and expressions of church. The individual parishioner already belongs to the same church at various levels in different ways: the universal level, the diocesan level and the parish level. The Small Church Community (SCC) would constitute yet another level. (Recent popes and the American bishops have spoken of an even more basic experience of church: the "foundational church" of the family.)

For a Catholic, belonging to the church at each level enhances the belonging at every other level. The parish level is where the Catholic tends to experience the church more personally in order to appreciate Catholic belonging beyond one's immediate experience. The parish, then, is where the universal church becomes a reality. Being a Catholic in the Small Church Community only enhances loyalty and commitment to the wider parish.

Two examples from St. Elizabeth Seton demonstrate this creative interplay between levels of church: First, SCC members, even people who had never been involved previously in the parish, responded without fail to meet the needs of the wider parish and of the world beyond the parish. Second, almost all the non-Catholic spouses of SCC members eventually came into the Catholic Church, in most cases with their entire small community serving as sponsors.

A Total Approach to Parish

Such a plan obviously does not mean the simple addition of small-group experiences for *some* parishioners while the parish as a whole continues as before. The pastoral plan—and overarching goal—is to move all parishioners to experience the church at this more basic level, but always respecting each person's pace.

Existing small-group programs within the parish can be helpful at various stages in the effort to create these basic

15

Catholic communities. *But the vision gets lost if this movement toward being church at a more basic level becomes just one more parish activity piled upon all the other parish activities.* Nor should this be seen as the answer for a few years until a better answer comes along. The decision to embark on the process described here is founded on a vision of what church at the parish level should be every year for everyone.

These Small Church Communities, therefore, are for *all* Catholic parishioners—not just the "religious types." They are intended to be permanent or semi-permanent and, eventually, to manifest all the activities of the larger church: worship, formation, service.

Now this goal demands hard work and is not achieved overnight, and, in fact, is never achieved once and for all. Motivating people to try a beginning program is always an ongoing challenge and the work of motivating is never finished. The three stages for a small group to develop into a church community take at least two years and each group grows at its own pace. New groups will always be beginning, too. The whole parish obviously does not go through this parish plan in lockstep.

Yet our basic conviction is that the church needs to begin existing at this more basic level and the parish needs to deliberately and methodically plan for this to happen. This means allowing the pastoral plan of restructuring to become the focus of all the other activities of the parish and insisting that it color the way the parish operates. (More on this in later chapters.)

The larger parish community and its pastoral leaders become more important—not less important—once this pastoral plan is set in motion. The Sunday parish Eucharist remains crucial, even more so than before, as the unifying experience of all these small communities. Likewise, parish religious formation programs for all ages are needed to provide the larger experience of church to complement the small church experience. And the small faith communities cannot be churches in any Catholic sense without strong pastoral links to the other levels of church. In no way, then, does this plan fracture or divide the parish.

16

The Pastoral Bridge

The name for the leader of the Small Church Communities communicates the vision that the small faith community is indeed the church. The leader is called a *pastoral facilitator (PF)*. The heart of this title is the word *pastoral*, an adjective used only about leadership in the church. Even if another member serves as facilitator, or if members take turns facilitating (which is recommended), only one person or couple *pastors* the community. Prayer groups, faith-sharing groups, Scripture-study groups: all can have facilitators, but only a church has a pastor!

Each level of the Catholic Church is linked to the new level of church by a pastoral person. The bishop, for example, links the Church of Detroit to the universal church by his communion with his brother bishops and the Bishop of Rome. The pastor is the bridge between a parish (the Church of St. Elizabeth Seton) and the local diocesan church. Thus the pastoral facilitator is a connector between the base church (the Small Church Community that meets every other Wednesday at the Zabrinskis') and the pastor/pastoral staff of a particular parish. Without this pastoral connection, even though all the very same sharing and activity goes on, the group is not a complete base church.

Lots of parishes have small groups of interested parishioners meeting to share their faith, such as RENEW groups or Catholic Family Movement groups. These groups can develop into—but are not yet—"the church in miniature." This does not happen until a pastoral network is operative to link the small groups to the larger church.

We are Catholic—and not *congregational*—because of the way we are linked pastorally to every level of church. Clearly, then, what makes this pastoral plan a restructuring of the parish church, and not only parishioners getting together in small support groups, is the pastoral linkage established between these small groups and the larger church. This pastoral link— the pastoral facilitator—helps keep a Small Church Community from self-absorption, insulation, isolation, elitism. The selection and formation of these pastoral leaders is treated in Chapter Four.

'You Brought Us Together'

Bringing people together is why the parish exists and restructuring into smaller parish communities brings people together better. This parish vision is not just so much theory. It is rooted in the everyday lives of ordinary Catholic parishioners at St. Elizabeth Seton Parish where this plan was formulated and put into action.

St. Elizabeth Seton has 600 households, mostly couples in their late 30's with both spouses working, some older people, high transiency, no parish school, recreational and social activities for children sponsored by the city, adults commuting to work, parents finishing degree work. In short: modern secular, suburban America where hectic life-styles and fast-paced lives are the rule of thumb. The operating priority of most of these people 10 years ago would not have been to become better Catholics or to connect everyday life and faith in a Small Church Community.

After 10 years the parish has 250 people in 34 Small Church Communities. Now there are 250 personal stories to put flesh and blood on this vision. The two testimonies that follow are uncoached and unabridged. I asked these people to speak about their experience because neither person is the typical involved parishioner who joins groups in a parish.

This first story speaks of giving back to others after the experience of the small community. The second gets to the heart of the Small Church Community: the way ordinary Catholic people in an ordinary parish deeply affect each other and the parish in their everyday lives.

A S T O R Y

I am a 32-year-old mother of two children, married for 11 years. I had been away from the church since marriage and joined the parish after our second child was born, basically to have her baptized. How's that for coming back for the wrong reason!

I was raised by parents who were nonpracticing themselves. I never went to a Catholic school. The difference my small community has made for me personally is not having to struggle alone so much. The SCC really did change my life. I wish I could talk about this more easily, but it is still very hard for me. So I write.

Being a part of our group and sharing their struggles and feeling their trust and love gave me the courage and the push that I needed to come to Confession. It did change my life. I will be forever grateful to them for that. Sometimes it feels like a dream. I lived with that pain and guilt for so long with no one to talk to about it and then, when I finally did go to Confession, it was like a great weight was lifted. Sometimes I can't believe that I really did it or that it made so much difference just to finally get it all out. Now the real work begins. That had so totally overshadowed everything that I couldn't think about anything else. It really was my excuse for everything that was wrong in my life and was, in that sense, hard to let go. Now it is time to move on to other things and that's scary—but I now do have hope that I can figure things out. How did I live without the people of my small community!

God sent me here to the parish and to this group for all of this to take place, of that I am sure. He put all of these people in my path and, because of that, I know God must love me a lot. If I can just give a little bit of what I have received back, I'll be happy.

ANOTHER STORY

My name is Romeo; I am 37 years old. I still cannot believe I am writing about my experience as a Catholic or that anyone would be interested enough to listen to my experience of the church.

First of all, I've been a Catholic all my life but never went to church that much. The family I came from went to Mass sometimes. In the large parish where I was raised, church was a place you went to. Secondly, I'm a quiet type of person and keep more to myself. My view on being a Catholic began to change three winters ago with an argument my wife had with me before work. Anna told me she didn't know if she wanted to stay married to me. My life fell apart that day. We had three

19

small children, one not yet in school. I had been doing all the right things learned in an ethnic home, like being very responsible and working long hours. At 7:30 a.m. on a weekday morning, I had to talk to someone. I couldn't go to work because I was so upset.

I went to the parish house to talk to Father Art because I had no other friends then. I had nowhere else to turn. Two years later our marriage is still together and I've (we've) changed our priorities and our views. We didn't go to a marriage counselor but joined a small group at church with other couples like us and with two single adults, too. I joined reluctantly, and for a long time I didn't say much. But Father Art asked me to come to the first six meetings of the group before I dropped out.

I'm really not a joiner of groups. I actually needed more than those six sessions to get comfortable with the small group. Now these people in our small group are our friends. They care about us and about our marriage, and they pray for us. The couples in our small community understand the kind of struggles my wife and I face because they, too, need to review their family priorities, ask questions about falling into the same old pattern of work and responsibility, and also to know God is there for them in their marriage.

We didn't need a marriage counselor. I know some couples do, but Anna and I needed people to care about us and talk about the way we were living.

When Father Art was leaving our parish, our little community had him over to say good-bye. We made a special evening to tell Father how much he made a difference in our lives. After a skit and a roast, we got serious. Anna and I stood in front of Father when it was our turn. I asked him if he remembered when I came to see him two years earlier about my life and marriage. "I didn't know these people then," I said. "You were the only one I could go to."

I told him how grateful we were because of these people he got us together with. My life has truly changed because of the people of our small group. "You brought us together," I said. "I really didn't know any of these people two years ago. Now, they are like family."

Today Romeo might not have to come to see me or any

parish staff because he and Anna have these fellow Catholics as a prayerful support. The people of the base church actually minister to each other instead of depending on the staff or the priest of the parish to handle everything. The most important work of the staff is to find a way to bring people together to be church for each other.

I think Romeo's statement that I brought people together is the highest compliment I can be paid as a pastor. It is not what I can do as one individual for other individuals in my parish, but what I can enable them to do for each other.

After answering the following questions for yourself, decide on two people in your parish you will ask these questions of:

How much of what happens in your parish depends directly on the parish staff? Where would a person like Romeo turn for help in your parish?

Name the ways parishioners do experience each other as church. What two people will you ask these questions of?

Summing Up

Bringing the people of your parish together in small church communities is not the only way to be church. I am, however, convinced that it is the most effective way. I am writing this book to try to convince interested parishioners, pastoral staffs and pastors that: (1) Small Church Communities are possible in most, if not all, parishes; (2) the average pastor or staff person is capable of effecting this parish restructuring; (3) restructuring your parish into small communities is well worth the effort.

Calling people together to be church for each other is hard work and demands a steady effort over many years. There are no magic or immediate results. But the process is worth our best efforts, for through it parishioners revitalize each other, the staff and the parish in an ongoing way.

The rest of this book will attempt to explain how all the

existing aspects of parish life are affected by this pastoral plan—and to outline the practical steps any parish can take to move in this direction.

CHAPTER TWO

From Vision to Reality in Your Parish

*I*n order to move your parish toward the vision described in the preceding pages, you need a parish plan with clear steps that deliberately moves the parish toward its ultimate goal. This plan must put into perspective all the everyday emergencies and demands, help determine how important the present variety of parish activities really is in the grand scheme of things and allow the better use of parishioner and staff time and talent.

The Catholic Church in the United States had such a parish plan for much of its history. The goal of this plan was the creation of a tight-knit parish around a parish school. The plan was clear and tangible (brick and mortar). And it was successful. Catholics exerted great energy and made many sacrifices in the service of its clearly stated goal.

But where are we going today? Is there a present plan for our parish life? Some parishes seem only to be on a maintenance plan. This caretaker philosophy provides services and makes sacraments available. But no new way of envisioning the parish is involved. Other parishes develop innovative approaches to parish life and ministry, but these plans last only as long as the innovative staff member or priest stays in the parish.

Many other parishes wear out staffs and the same pool of volunteers with too many activities and programs, while the rest of the parishioners show up to receive the services of the few.

Does your parish have a long-range plan? What is it? Does this plan provide a rationale for all your parish activities?

Does your parish need a new plan?

A Three-Phase Process

Making the vision of Small Church Communities—base churches—a reality in your parish demands a plan. In order to construct a realistic plan for your parish, you need to know the three phases a group goes through to become a base church. These three phases do not necessarily proceed in some rigid order and a phase does not begin or end at some precise point. Rather, the three phases are three experiences necessary for the small community to grow and mature. (Much more will be said about each phase in Chapters Three and Five.)

Phase One: A Beginning Experience. The first phase is a "beginning experience" in a small group with eight to 12 people who communicate honestly and value each other. This experience can be provided in a number of ways. RENEW was one way to introduce large numbers of parishioners to such a small-group experience.

Come As You Are (available from the National Alliance) is a program specifically designed to provide this beginning experience.

The beginning experience has often already occurred in a parish and may be the very reason why the pastoral staff or certain parishioners are thinking in new ways about what it means to be church, what it means to be parish. How often we heard the remark: "We just finished RENEW. Now what?"

The important requirement is that the beginning experience, whatever format is adopted, bring participants together weekly. The goal is to foster a sense of belonging to the group and to help members develop these skills: listening to others, paying attention to one's own experience and priorities, and self-affirmation.

The Phase One program should provide the following:
• good group dynamics, using smaller groupings of

twos and threes
- an easy format to allow more than one person to facilitate
- a practice in listening and content based more on life experience than "church talk."

Phase Two: Praying Alone and Together. The second phase, or "second experience," focuses on prayer. At St. Elizabeth Seton we developed our own 11-session process to encourage small-group participants to pray regularly alone and together. This process, *Praying Alone and Together: An 11-Session Prayer Module for Small Faith Communities*, is available from St. Anthony Messenger Press. You could also use Mark Link's *Challenge 2000*, available from Tabor Publishing, as a basic format. The goal of Phase Two is to bring people together every two weeks to practice the art of listening and responding to God's moment-to-moment revelation in ourselves, others and the world around us. This workshop on prayer aims to increase reverence for life—especially one's own life.

Phase Three: Being Church for the Long Haul. At the end of Phase Two, the group begins to identify itself specifically as "church." This book (*Creating Small Church Communities*) can be used and discussed by members as part of the input for group meetings during Phase Three. The members make an agreement and evaluate their community as church. (See Appendices B and C for samples.)

By now, a group member has received pastoral facilitator training from the parish staff. (See the accompanying book, *Pastoring the 'Pastors'*, available from St. Anthony Messenger Press.) This pastoral facilitator now connects the small community to the larger parish.

The Phase Three community meets regularly. Weekly is too often for many people and monthly is too seldom for a community to remain strong. Meeting every two weeks seems the best pattern.

Summary: Called to Be Church Process

	PHASE ONE *The Beginning Experience*	PHASE TWO *The Prayer Module*	PHASE THREE *The Church Community*
GOAL	Eight to 12 people taking time —to communicate —to value each other —to belong to each other	Eight to 12 people supporting each other in a commitment —to pray alone —to pray together	A small community confirming its identity —by connecting with the church's story —by reaching out in service
SKILLS	Listening Paying attention to life Identifying priorities Self-affirmation	Praying, defined as: "The art of listening and responding to God revealing himself moment by moment"	Learning the church's story Creating good focus questions for Scripture-sharing
FORMAT	RENEW *Come As You Are*	*Praying Alone and Together* Mark Link's Challenge Program or Action 2000 Program	Two-Hour Format for the Church Community (see page 75) • *Faith Sharing for Small Church Communities* • *Quest*
MEETINGS	Weekly	Every two weeks	Every two weeks

26

The format for Phase Three grows out of Thomas Groome's model of shared praxis. At each meeting the Small Church Community uses the Sunday Scriptures as a way to look at their own lives and experience. This looking at life through Scripture and Tradition is done with the help of specifically prepared focus questions. (More on this in Chapter Five.) Members try to connect their individual faith experience and the life experience of the society and culture in which they live with the experience of the church in Scripture and Tradition. The goal of this phase is to support the small church for the long haul.

It is in Phase Three that we can really begin to speak of the small faith community as a "base church." There isn't any Phase Four because Phase Three is the mode for indefinitely continuing to live and renew one's Catholic Christianity.

This three-phase process is summarized in the chart on page 26. The rest of this book will now zero in on specific issues in adopting and implementing this plan in your parish.

Resources for each of the phases are listed in Appendix A on page 101.

Appendix E includes the stages of psychological growth that any group moves through on the journey to becoming a community and helpful responses at each stage.

A Long-Term Commitment

Before we proceed with the nuts and bolts, I want to reiterate an earlier point. No matter how strongly you embrace the vision of transforming your parish into a community of Small Church Communities, it won't happen overnight. It takes careful, realistic planning and commitment for the long haul.

How fast your parish can move depends on many things: your parish history, previous small-group experiences, the present level of faith-sharing by the staff and by parishioners. Each parish must, to some extent, find its own way. Whether you are a parishioner, a staff person or the pastor, the better you know the particulars of your parish, the better able you will be to shape a good plan for how to proceed.

The basic steps outlined in the next section can get you

started. The planner, however, needs to move slowly and thoughtfully! The parish composed of Small Church Communities results from a long process needing a long-term commitment.

First Steps

By this point I am assuming that you are attracted to the vision presented here and have shared this vision with a few other people in your parish who are also enthused. Now what? Here are eight basic steps to help you get started on the gradual process to a restructured parish:

1) Identify key people/form a core team.
2) Assess your parish.
3) Start with the experience.
4) Include several area parishes.
5) Consider a two-and-a-half-day workshop with the National Alliance.
6) Start small and set realistic goals.
7) Color the entire parish with your vision.
8) Commit to consistent leadership.

Now let's take a closer look at each of these steps.

Identifying Key People/Forming a Core Team

A plan becomes the parish plan by convincing the parish leaders. The designated leaders include pastor, pastoral associates, staff, parish council, parish commissions and so on. But other parishioners play leadership roles (even though not in a designated way) because they can motivate people or influence certain groups within the parish. Identifying the leaders, official and unofficial, and sharing the vision and the plan with them is key. This leadership base is the best hope of making the vision of church communities the accepted vision of the parishioners themselves.

One good way to share the vision with your key people is to show the 35-minute video 20/20 Vision for the Parish, A Clear Direction for the Future and use the study guide (available from the National Alliance). In this video parishioners and staff from restructuring parishes speak of their experience and their enthusiasm. A more thorough and detailed resource with discussion questions built in is the 90-minute video *Creating Small Faith Communities* (St. Anthony Messenger Press).

Who are the "key people" in your parish?

Who are the best people:

> *to articulate clearly the vision of restructuring the church— and to keep articulating it?*

> *to motivate parishioners to try an initial group experience?*

> *to find the best programs to get people comfortable with each other and to begin to share?*

> *to identify leaders, potential facilitators?*

> *to keep calling everyone back to the vision and the plan and their commitments to it?*

Some of the key people you identify should form a core team with the pastor to make this plan happen. This core team must stay small enough (eight to 12 people) to be able to communicate with each other well and to work closely together. (In a small parish this core team could be smaller.) The core team should eventually include at least one pastoral facilitator, once the parish is far enough along to have pastoral facilitators.

The core team gets started by simply reading and discussing this book. Then they work through the remaining six steps outlined below.

Gradually this core team will come to share faith and pray together in order to keep a clear vision for the parish community over the years the team continues to assess the progress of the parish, identify new key people, motivate parishioners to begin, support the ongoing Small Church Communities, help a new pastor or associate pastor experience the Small Church Community process, and so on. Even though individual members will need to be replaced at times, the team itself must be permanent because the restructuring plan is ongoing.

Which of the key people identified above would make a good core team for your parish?

Assessing Your Parish

There is no one-and-only way to begin to restructure a particular parish into Small Church Communities. What helps one parish community arrive at the ultimate objective will not work in another parish because parishioners and staff are different. The whole point of restructuring is to make church more personal and experiential—not to impose some kind of blueprint upon people from above. Right from the start, therefore, it is critical to take the time to know the people of your parish. Parish history, ethnic and racial groups, types of neighborhoods—all of these influence how to proceed and the timing of the steps.

In one crime-ridden, inner-city Milwaukee parish (St. Thomas Aquinas) where people were afraid even to allow others into their homes, realistic planning demanded that a way be found to build trust among parishioners. Therefore, a series of neighborhood missions—or retreats—was initiated as the first beginning experience.

The following story from a multi-ethnic and multi-racial parish in Pontiac, Michigan, illustrates the need to adapt the process to your particular situation. Note the resources in Spanish in the bibliography in the back of the book.

A S T O R Y

I am Hispanic, born in Argentina, and I have lived in the United States for 20 years. I became a citizen. I presently work at St. Vincent de Paul Parish in Pontiac, Michigan. Our parish is very mixed with Anglos, Blacks and Hispanics. The Hispanics are more than 50 percent with a majority being Mexican

Americans as well as some Puerto Ricans and Central and South Americans.

Our parish has been committed to the idea of small communities since 1984. I myself have facilitated an English-speaking group for three years. The growth and life that this experience gave me made me want to share it with the Hispanics in the community.

But small groups have to consider the differences in people. What may work with some may not work with others. So last Advent season I decided to try something.

We had a Novena to Our Lady of Guadalupe, but instead of nine consecutive days we did it for nine weeks. There are five Hispanic deacons in the parish and each one facilitated one group. Each met at a different home each time and the statue of the Virgin was moved from house to house.

I prepared the materials for each week. The format included singing, prayer and three or four discussion questions. Lots of people participated and the evaluations were favorable. Some groups continued meeting during the year, and all groups prepared something special for the day of Our Lady, December 12. We had an especially nice celebration.

In Lent, I used the same approach, but this time I made tapes with songs in Spanish fitting for Lent. In place of Mary we had a small altar with a crucifix in each home (a family crucifix if possible) and a candle. The questions were directed to the special circumstances of our Hispanic community.

Senior citizens and people without transportation were picked up by others. The experience was wonderful. New people started coming to church. We had Baptisms, First Communions, new children for religious education. The deacons have also gained confidence with this small-group approach.

I have hopes this will be just a beginning for us and that, in the future, most of our people will be members of small communities.

What special circumstances in your parish would have to be taken into account in moving toward base churches?

31

What positive or negative small-group experiences have to be factored into any plan?

Starting With the Experience

No one can be a truly effective member of the Core Team without, at the same time, being a member of an SCC. So, the first step in planning the parish may be to begin a few groups with some good prospects for the future Core Team scattered around as members of these beginning groups. After completing the Phase One program, these prospects are asked to form the Core Planning Team, while they continue as members (not as the pastoral facilitators) of the ongoing groups.

The first step of the Core Team's formation is the study—chapter by chapter—of this book *Creating Small Church Communities*. The video and study guide *20/20 Vision For the Parish* is also helpful. The six sessions of the pastoral facilitator training book *Pastoring the Pastors* are a good formation process for the Core Team, as well. And, of course, each Core Team meeting includes time for life/faith sharing and prayer.

There are two reasons why this experiential approach is so important: (1) Leaders need to know how the small-group experience slowly builds, as well as what helps and hinders the group along the way. (2) Leaders will motivate others—that is, "sell" more convincingly—because they have seen what ordinary Catholic people can do for each other in this kind of structure.

Putting all staff, parish council members, core team and/or other leadership people together in one initial group is probably not the way to begin. Such an atypical group will give little indication of how things will go with ordinary parishioners, and leadership people will be limited to these few groups when their leadership is needed in other small beginning groups. Better to start by grouping several leadership people with parishioners of different ages and stages of life. There is no need for people to know each other beforehand. Eight to 12 is a good number for interaction. Your first year will be a success if you can get a few groups—or even one—to move together through whatever format you envision for Phase One and Phase Two in your parish plan. Even though some parish staff and council people may have already had the experience of sharing faith and prayer in a small group, it is important that they begin in a group on a par with the ordinary parishioner. Being a member, and not the group's facilitator, helps too. Certain Phase-One formats, such as *Come As You Are*, are easily facilitated by the average person with no previous exposure to groups, and different group members can take turns facilitating.

By the second year these "graduates" will be the best spokespersons for the parish plan of Small Church Communities. They can also become the planners of the next steps for the total parish.

Are you—and fellow enthusiasts for base churches—speaking from experience? What experience?

If not, how can you structure a beginning experience for yourself before tackling the larger parish?

What Phase-One format (see chart on page 26) seems to best fit your situation?

Including Several Area Parishes

If a few parishes in a diocese or the same part of a state concurrently pursue the pastoral objective of reorganizing into Small Church Communities, they can be an obvious help to each other: Practical information can be shared. Each can help the others stay on course and avoid getting sidetracked by day-to-day demands, crises and emergencies of the moment. Each can also be helped by the others through transition times when a pastor or key staff person leaves the parish.

The overriding reason, however, for a cluster of area parishes to pursue this plan together is the Catholic Church. The whole point of reorganizing into smaller communities is to help the church become the best it can be. And the only way this plan will spread is if it is perceived as something that can work in many kinds of parishes—not just as an isolated experiment in a few parishes.

In several areas of the United States and Canada, clusters of parish pastors and staffs have already met, usually for two to three days, to investigate this pastoral plan together. Subsequent area meetings then follow on a regular basis to provide support and reinforcement. There now is a national organization to support and train parishes for restructuring. The National Alliance of Parishes Restructuring Into Communities (NAPRC) provides workshops for five or more area parishes moving in this direction. (Contact NAPRC, 1000 Michigan Ave., Marysville, MI 48040-1466, 810-364-3500.)

Starting Small and Setting Realistic Goals

One important key to success is to foresee what consequences will follow in a year from whatever first steps the parish takes. Every small community formed now will need a pastoral leader a year from now, and the leader will need initial training and ongoing formation. (See *Pastoring the 'Pastors': Resources for Training and Supporting Pastoral Facilitators for Small Faith Communities*, available from St. Anthony Messenger Press.) The parish staff will have to be involved in this training and formation—which means that some other parish activities may need to be curtailed. Being prepared to curtail these activities is being realistic.

For an already overworked or a very compartmentalized staff to begin 60 to 70 small groups all at once could doom the whole plan from the start. Five initial groups, who become the spokespeople to interest other parishioners to try the experience the next year, could be more workable. Or, in some parishes, simply sharing the idea with the pastor and one small group may take the bulk of one's effort for awhile. This is starting small.

But starting small and setting realistic goals does not mean doing nothing and never starting. The final objective—the whole parish restructured into base churches—can seem overwhelming and cause paralysis. The ultimate realism is to begin *one step at a time*, letting that one step lead to the next and the next and the next.

A STORY

I'm Father Dick Kelly. I've been pastor of a working-class, long-established parish of 1,100 families for seven years—and I've been the only priest. We have different ages and a large group of Mexican-Americans. There are lots of calls at the rectory door for all kinds of help.

What I like best about this parish restructuring plan is that it's *possible* for "tired old ministers." We are swamped by the day-to-day demands of ministry, often the demands of the moment. The restructuring does not just add more programs to get done and cause further burn-out. It gets away from having to relate directly to each person in the parish and gets people to relate to each other.

I also like the fact that this parish plan is "on-the-job training": You learn how to run groups by first going through as a group member. You learn to form pastoral leaders of the small communities by following the basic steps outlined in this plan. As you follow these steps, they become part of you and you pastor differently.

Most "front line" pastoral people don't have time to read lots of theory. This hands-on process, following five or six points and filling in between the lines, is what we need. We get formed ourselves by the doing.

Why haven't I restructured my parish into small basic communities? Last Lent we had many small groups meeting to share on the Sunday readings. They used experiential focus questions and prayed. But when Lent was over, so were the groups. It was the usual story—the everyday pace and the fact that it's easier to go by the call of the moment. But it was a beginning. The parish got used to small sharing groups.

Are we going into small communities parish-wide? I'm all for it. This time I've begun differently. My staff and I have begun to meet weekly using a beginning program. After two sessions, we are saying something more about ourselves to each other.

So *I'm* all for it; but I know myself and I know how the parish business can absorb a pastor. Maybe the staff will be convinced enough after our beginning program to stay on one main course. In our place it will take the whole staff to keep each other from getting lost in everything else going on.

Complete these statements:

    The best assets our parish has to begin restructuring are...

    The best assets I have to begin this plan are...

    The greatest challenges to face in our parish before we could begin this plan are...

    The greatest challenges to face in myself before beginning this plan are...

Whom would you ask to help you begin?

What keeps you from beginning?

Coloring the Parish

Once Small Church Communities become the parish goal, then this vision should color everything else that goes on in the parish. Parishioners not yet in small communities can begin to appreciate the life of the small church in every parish group, even the finance commission or the festival committee.

The consistent question to keep asking about every parish event—the ushers' meeting, a wake, choir practice—is this: How can these people here and now help each other connect their everyday life experience with faith? Parishioners and pastoral leaders gradually begin to do the regular work of the parish in a different way as they continually assess every parish event around the question of experiencing church.

The following are concrete efforts made at St. Elizabeth Seton to "color the parish." These new approaches were applied to the old, everyday activities that go on in every parish. They worked at our parish because they became, with dogged persistence, a way of operating:

• We took time for people to meet with each other and learn each others' names, even at busy task-oriented meetings.

36

Sometimes this meant apologizing for a seemingly silly name game, but we also explained our purpose.

• Various parishioners, rather than pastoral staff, would articulate how a certain activity helped us fulfill our mission as church. Sometimes short testimonies would be given at Mass.

• We began each parish council and commission meeting with faith sharing around a focus question based on Scripture. After hearing the question, people were given some quiet time to reflect. Then the large group broke into groups of three or four to share their responses. After coming back to the large group, there was an opportunity for large-group sharing and spontaneous prayer. This entire process need only take 20 to 30 minutes.

• At meetings of lectors, Eucharistic ministers, greeters and ushers, we always created an opportunity for sharing in a small group with fellow ministers on a question such as, "Can you name one way that being a lector has affected your own faith?"

• At the meeting to plan the parish picnic, we began with several moments of quiet, just letting ourselves relax in God's presence. Then each person on the planning committee was encouraged to express in a prayer of petition what good things they hoped would happen for our parishioners through the picnic.

• At a wedding rehearsal we gathered everyone around the bride and groom and encouraged them to pray out loud for what they believed the couple needed from God for their marriage. In conclusion all joined hands and prayed the Lord's Prayer.

• During parish Baptisms, family and friends were given a chance during the liturgy to write down individual prayers in this form: "My prayer for you on the day of your Baptism is...." some would be read aloud. An occasion like this can make it easier for parishioners to share faith in a personal way with each other.

• Confirmation parents and sponsors were asked to write the same kind of letter to the young person about to be confirmed.

• Our parish program for high school students, after a large-group session for input, always broke up into the same small groups of eight to 12 with the same adult couple as facilitators. The small group fostered a sense of trust and belonging, and the trained facilitators kept the focus of the group on the students' real experiences and putting these experiences in a faith context.

• Our parent religious education program always included time for reflective questions and small-group sharing.

• The major parish Lenten program was a six-week program for small groups focusing on the Sunday readings.

• Parish-wide missions or retreats always afforded parishioners the opportunity to reflect in small groups following each presentation. The suggested resolutions at the retreat closing always included signing up for a beginning experience based on a program such as *Come As You Are*. (Many who were not in existing groups did begin the small-group experience after such a retreat.)

• Newcomers to the parish were asked to attend a pre-registration meeting. A panel of four parishioners, including the pastor, articulated the parish vision, especially the parish plan for small communities. The opening prayer was always presented by a lay panelist.

All of the above are examples of trying to be consistent with the Small Church Community mentality in running the entire parish. The goal of the Small Church Community—that is, belonging, sharing one's faith and prayer together—can and should be realized to some degree at every parish gathering.

Leading Consistently

In every parish, no matter how hard people try to let the vision of Small Church Communities color every aspect of parish life and no matter how faithfully they move through the various phases of their plan, crisis can and will strike: The church burns down, or the organist resigns amidst great parishioner upset, or who knows what.

Crises test consistent leadership. Can the parish leaders recognize these crises for the distractions that they are, deal with them in an appropriate way, but then get back on course?

To help themselves stay on course, the leaders in the parish must be consistent about articulating the vision of the base churches. They need to be clear and to keep taking opportunities (in public situations, at dinner with parish families, at meetings, with individuals) to reiterate this basic direction.

Here are some special leadership challenges to be met along the way:

For staff. If there is a parish staff, part of the staff's role must be to assess how they operate their parish programs. Are they giving people in their programs a little quiet reflection time on everyday life and faith and then an opportunity to hear each other in small groups of three or four? In this way the staff keeps articulating the parish plan to each other. The other essential staff responsibility is to model the basic experience of church by sharing faith and learning to pray together regularly.

For the parish council. For the parish council, consistent leadership means clearly spelling out the goals and objectives of the parish. If reorganizing the parish into Small Church Communities is listed as just one parish goal among many others, the whole plan is relativized and no longer the priority. The parish council must communicate that restructuring is the focus of the parish or the way all the other parish goals can best be accomplished.

For example, full and active participation in the liturgy is a very worthwhile parish goal. But the best way to accomplish it may be by continuing to develop Small Church Communities. The goal of restructuring can refocus that worship goal in several ways: (1) by helping parishioners extend themselves to others on Sunday because they now know the experience of belonging in the church community; (2) by fostering reverence because people in the Small Church Community deepen their awareness of God in everyday life; and (3) by internalizing the meaning of the Sunday Scriptures as small communities share the Sunday readings in their meetings.

Through belonging to a Small Church Community, people gradually change their attitudes, values and hearts before they ever arrive at the Sunday Eucharist. Until that happens, all the specific liturgical changes are limited in achieving full and active participation.

The other consideration in articulating the parish plan is the tendency of councils—and staffs—to keep adding more good programs to the parish's life. The problem is that each good program takes the time and energy of involved parishioners and usually of the staff. The other problem is that this proliferation of programs leaves the parish with no clear-cut, basic direction to unify it. Each parishioner can have his or her own ideas on which is most important of all these programs. The only unifier is usually an ideal mission statement saying something like this: "We are the church making Jesus present through our fellowship, worship, formation and service." But this pastoral plan for creating Small Church Communities takes that general mission statement and sets a practical way to live as the church.

The parish council needs to plan the parish not to be better, but to be different; the video *20/20 Vision For the Parish* and its study guide are very useful in helping the council and staff to imagine the parish differently.

For all leaders. To lead consistently you must *be consistent with yourself.* Take time to reflect on the events of your own life—and where the Lord might be in the process. Look for some way to share your own faith experiences in some group or with a few others.

Do you have a clear, specific goal that gives direction to your life? Your ministry?

Do you see a need to grow in being consistent? What is a single specific step you are willing to take? Can you share this with anyone?

Given your present role in the parish, what kind of consistent leadership can you undertake to advance this plan?

How reflective are you? With whom do you—or can you—speak a bit about your life journey?

CHAPTER THREE

From Small Groups Toward Small Church Communities

A small group develops over a period of time into a church. The next three chapters trace this three-phase development process and focus on the mechanics for getting a group together and keeping it together. In this chapter we will talk about the first two phases in this process of small-group transformation.

Groups: Getting Started

The ideal size of a Small Church Community is from eight to 12 members. Experts in group process say that at least eight members are necessary for good interaction patterns, and any more than 12 make it too easy for an individual not to feel missed. Besides, a home cannot usually accommodate more than this number!

Who Groups With Whom? First it's important to say how *not* to group people: by age, by interest of any kind or because they live next door. The goal is always a community of diversity. Accommodations will always have to be made—for example, the group of elderly parishioners in a retirement home who may only be able to group with each other.

But the vision of the base church as a cross section of the big church should never be surrendered.

Why not next door neighbors? At least in Anglo parishes, neighbors often are not comfortable in a closer relationship and want a certain distance from each other, but are perfectly willing to join with other parishioners in a beginning group. However, dividing up a large parish into sections and having small communities composed of people living in those sections is being tried in a few places. Our approach at St. Elizabeth Seton, and the most common approach around the United States and Canada, is to form the group around the time when people are available to meet. All the people who can meet on Tuesday evening form the Tuesday night group or groups. One grouping doomed from the start in our parish was composed of five couples, casually acquainted with each other and living on two adjoining streets. Two of the wives thought that the combination was a natural, but most of these particular neighbors wanted to keep their neighborhood relationship just as it was and felt uncomfortable with more. The group never bonded; people found excuses early on to miss meetings. Two of the couples later joined other groups and persevered.

Why not by interest? Because the church itself is not built on interest. All charismatics, all Catholic school parents, all justice and peace activists, all those with a special interest in Scripture, all whatever—none of these interest groups reflects the diversity of the church. All these groups and more—widowed groups, divorced groups and young adult groups—certainly can continue in the parish restructured into small communities. But these groups continue as authentic special interest groups and not as base churches.

Grouping people on the basis of age or sex is also not the ideal expression of church. Daytime groups of women or of senior citizens may be an accommodation to a particular parish circumstance because nothing else is workable. Yet the goal is always a community of diversity.

When you are ready to begin, simply ask people to sign up for a particular evening or day of the week, indicating a second preference. Coordinators can then form groups on the basis of chosen times with these additional concerns factored in: (1) Supporting "minority" members. (We tried to place at least two "minority" people together in the same group. "Minority," of course, would mean different things in different groups: single persons, couples, men or women, foreign-born, elderly.) (2) Including at least one potential pastoral facilitator. (3) Achieving a good mix of personalities and backgrounds.

The core team, the staff, or other parishioners who know the parish as well as understand the vision of base churches can decide on the groups' membership. There is no need for people to know each other beforehand and, in fact, previous familiarity and an already achieved acquaintance level can hinder interaction.

Motivating Parishioners

Most parishioners are not going to respond to a mass appeal to share their faith with eight to 12 other adults. Many Catholics have never prayed spontaneously and "sharing faith" can sound awfully religious. Most people are not all that self-confident, and talking about God in personal terms is just beyond many Catholics at the start.

Being with new people or people known only superficially is quite difficult enough. Starting with a very religious-sounding program will cause many Catholics to exclude themselves from the start. Besides, many of our people lead busy and demanding lives, already too full of commitments.

The best initial motivation is an appeal to the everyday life and needs of parishioners which asks for a limited time commitment. If parishioners perceive that you are asking them to commit to an ongoing group where getting out will be difficult, then few people will ever begin. People need to take one step—and one stage—at a time. At the end of each stage, group members can decide whether or not to continue for the next experience. All that is asked at the beginning is to commit to an initial program, and *not* to a Small Church Community. Our hope is that the people in the group will pull together and want to remain together for an ongoing life.

If the *Come As You Are* program is used, the initial "pitch" to people can easily focus on genuine self-interest, such as clarifying priorities (what really counts) in one's life;

discovering how to live better in the present and enjoy life more; developing a more positive attitude about oneself and others, a greater contentment with each day, a fuller awareness of everyday life, a deeper sense of God's love. These generalities can be made real and credible through parishioner testimonials at Mass and elsewhere. Other initial programs include a definite step-by-step plan to motivate parishioners to join.

The care of the staff, the friendliness of the parish and the parish emphasis on life reflection and learning to listen to each other at every parish activity contribute to motivating parishioners to respond to the request. But the single most effective way to encourage a person to join a group will always be the personal invitation.

As parishioners experience the Small Church Community, they can call fellow parishioners to invite them to try an initial easy program. These parishioners can also give testimonies at Mass and put on information evenings. If a parish is only beginning, however, the pastor, the staff and the core team members will have to do the motivating.

Another starting point could be a renewal weekend put on at the parish. There are several available retreat weekend formats which parish teams direct in their own parishes. On the parish retreat, the parishioners experience a real bond with each other through the witness talks, personal reflection and speaking and listening in small groups. After the retreat, people are quite willing to continue in a Phase One small group program.

The newly baptised and those received into full communion at Easter are another group who have experienced life reflection in a community through the RCIA process. These new Catholics need an ongoing experience of church community. Some of their formation actually could happen in existing Small Church Communities of which they would remain a part. Or, after Easter these new Catholics could join with a mix of regular parishioners beginning a Phase One group.

In most parishes a variety of motivational approaches will be used over the years because different people respond to different appeals. Since new groups need to be starting up continually, there is no foreseeable end to motivating people.

Phase One: Focus on Belonging

The initial experience, whatever the particular format for beginning, aims to get people comfortable with each other so they can begin to share what they are thinking and feeling. In short, the goal is for members to *belong*, that is, know that others really want to get to know them better and will miss them if they are absent.

A false sense of what it means to be religious can be an obstacle for many parishioners in getting involved in a beginning experience. Organizers need to stress that you can "be religious without being religious." So many of us hold an image of a religious person as always unruffled by the stresses of life, always kind and giving, always praying, knowing the Bible, having special experiences of God. Most ordinary Catholics, however, do not identify with this image. Nor have they ever experienced God in a dramatic way. They therefore conclude they are not religious people. They live an ordinary life of job, family, kids, aging and financial concerns. To get into a religious group with religious people from church sounds like having to pretend "to be nice."

One early group at St. Elizabeth Seton included an Irish Catholic defending Holy Mother Church against all odds; two 40-year-old men who played devil's advocate about church issues to the embarrassment of their wives; a couple living together without marriage and deciding if being Catholic was part of their future; an agnostic non-Catholic, sincere and sensitive to others, married to a Catholic. Needless to say, this small community was not traditionally religious. The members were free to be themselves to the point that eventually the blood boiled about values and life-styles and a few tempers flared.

The group met for years, however, and the core still continues. The unmarried couple married in church with all of the group present. When the agnostic and his family moved to Chicago, the whole group visited over a weekend, camping on the floor in sleeping bags. Although he never formally entered the church, he did enter into a close association with Catholics and he also made a contribution to their lives. He certainly had access to a sense of belonging to the church in this small group in a way that the larger parish could not have provided for him. Another couple now in California keeps in touch and has been visited by members of the group who were vacationing or traveling for business.

How to be themselves and to appreciate each other—that's what this group learned. Something happened to the members of that Small Church Community over the months and years, and they were all different—and better—for it.

The strongest message to keep communicating as we motivate people to join a small group is this: The only requirement is to be willing to simply be yourself. You can say as much as you wish, or say nothing for a while. Listening to others, of course, is an absolute must.

The premise here is that God speaks through all people and through their everyday experiences. People have to be themselves with each other. Religiosity can get in the way of people being real with themselves. But real religion begins with each person appreciating the life he or she has, even with all the weaknesses, because the Lord communicates through that life. There is no question here of neglecting the church's moral stands or belief system. The beginning experience, however, has to create an environment of trust, openness and freedom. Therefore the program used has to keep people focused on life and life experiences and not become a study group or theology program.

Which Format? Any program[*] to get people together initially will do, as long as the environment of trust and openness is fostered. Many parishes have had or are in the process of small RENEW groups. RENEW began as a process of five semesters or "seasons," with six sessions each. RENEW's intention, however, was that these small groups continue afterward. The sense of belonging fostered by RENEW is time-tested and

---

[*]All programs and materials mentioned here and throughout are listed in Appendix A with publishers and addressess.

works. But six sessions at a time with breaks of several weeks' duration in between can be a weakness. Small groups build slowly. So breaking after six sessions may not be optimum. Weekly meetings are important in this first phase. Long intervals between get-togethers slows down the trust and care that must build. People are most likely to drop out of a group in the first year and during breaks. Keeping intervals between meetings short is most important.

The *Come As You Are* program was designed by a national writing team specifically as a Phase One program. Meant to be a beginning program of 12 sessions for people who have never been with each other in the group before, *Come As You Are* is used widely in parishes to start Small Church Communities. The program cuts across educational, cultural and economic barriers. It is available from the National Alliance. (See Appendix A.)

A Phase One program, like *Come As You Are*, has to get people feeling at home by speaking their everyday life experiences and learning to listen—listen to self, others, the wider world and people who are different. The group interaction has to be simple and easy. This listening, after all, is what will make listening to and hearing God possible.

The most common analyses at the program's conclusion use words to this effect: "You know, Father, I can't tell you what I got out of *Come As You Are*, but I really like the people of my group. I can say anything to them." Or, "I've said more about myself there than to my family." Or, "I never thought I'd be saying I liked belonging to a church group."

These comments say well what the beginning experience for the small community is all about: a sense of belonging and of making a difference to a particular group of people. This is the single most critical factor in a group's continuing and persevering.

Phase Two: Praying Alone and Together

Through a program such as *Come As You Are*, group members begin to belong to each other. They also begin to pay attention to their own experience and to feel comfortable sharing that experience with others. To notice one's life, even without bringing God into the process, is a big step for many people. Our culture does not encourage a reflective life-style. So, something quite significant is started in Phase One.

At the end of Phase One, however, a small group is still a small group—not the Small Church Community we are aiming for. That level of church will never develop without this beginning experience.

The second group experience builds on the accomplishments of Phase One: belonging, trusting, reflecting on life. Phase Two becomes more explicitly religious and focuses on praying both individually and communally.

Vincent Dwyer, the creator of the original *Genesis II*, makes this critical point: God is found or not found in the human. He defines spirituality as "the art of listening and responding to God revealing himself moment by moment." Another name for this art is prayer.

Learning to listen and respond to God is at the heart of Small Church Communities—and practicing this art is what keeps them from becoming just another study or discussion group. (It's a lot easier to talk about prayer than to pray.) The goal of Phase Two, therefore, is precisely to help a group of trusting people reflect more seriously on their lives by praying alone and together.

At St. Elizabeth Seton we developed an 11-session workshop on praying which we called the Prayer Module. As a group completed Phase One—whatever the format of the experience—they were invited to move into this second experience. This meant committing to meet every week for 11 weeks or every other week for about five months. We let each group decide what rhythm best suited members' lives. But groups do begin to lose cohesion when the interval between meetings is more than two weeks.

The materials we developed to move groups through this prayer experience are contained in *Praying Alone and Together:*

48

An 11-Session Prayer Module for Small Faith Communities
(available from St. Anthony Messenger Press). This book
contains resources both for group sessions as well as for private
prayer times between sessions. A special facilitator's section at
the end provides session outlines and suggestions so that
anyone can easily facilitate the group during this phase.

In the first sessions of this Prayer Module, listening and
responding to God is practiced through listening exercises,
praying with imagination, listening to Scripture, going over just
one day of one's life. Various activity sheets and discussion
questions are provided to help the group practice these and
other prayer skills.

Many Catholics are not comfortable praying aloud in their
own words. For awhile, therefore, the group prayer may simply
be a quiet time. Being comfortable with the quiet is important.
Other exercises make shared prayer easier by asking
participants to thank God for one gift or to pray for one need or
for one person.

Beginning with session four, participants are asked to
spend 10 minutes a day in some personal reflection or prayer.
Prayer exercises to assist participants in these daily prayer times
are provided. The discipline of daily prayer is stressed, and the
group meetings increasingly depend on individuals spending
time in prayer between the meetings.

Not everybody is motivated right away to make time each
day for individual reflection, nor do people easily continue this
practice.

There also is continuing difficulty in speaking about God
in a personal way. Yet, gradually, people do grow in prayer and
become more confident that they can "do it right" as they begin
to trust their own experiences. Prayer does not always mean
doing all the talking; it can mean letting the dialogue take place
or simply being available to the Lord. Because we don't
naturally pray or listen well, the group becomes a great
support. Hearing someone we have come to know over time
speak about his or her struggles to be open to God can motivate
us to keep trying.

Phase Two aims to help people pray as a group and as
individuals. The specific goals at this stage are: (1) to enable
people to recognize God communicating to them through their

experience; (2) to begin to talk about God in a personal way; and (3) to voice a prayer response in a group setting.

Praying Alone and Together may have too much material for each session. Therefore, the group should proceed at its own pace and not feel pressured to finish all the material listed for one session in one sitting. One session can be covered over two meetings' time, if appropriate.

The Pastoral Link

Before moving on to discuss Phase Three of the process from small group to base church, we need to stop for a closer look at pastoral facilitators—what they are, how they are selected and what kind of training they need. For pastoral facilitators in a restructuring parish provide that pastoral link which ties the base church into the larger parish and the universal church. Only when a pastoral facilitator is actually functioning can the Small Church Community properly be called a small church.

The next chapter will explain what pastoral facilitators are, how and when they are selected and the kind of ongoing training and support the parish needs to provide for them.

A STORY

I'm writing what follows for Charlie, because he is not comfortable with the English language. But it's *his* story. It is also the story of the progression of a Small Church Community.

Cedomir (we call him "Charlie") is a man in his 30's, raised in a Communist country where all his schooling was atheistic. In his small village, only a few older women continued to go to church. His own mother had made sure Charlie was baptized as an infant in the Orthodox Church, but, as he was growing up, religion was unimportant and really a joke.

Then, Charlie came to America. Like most immigrants from Europe, he is extremely hardworking and struggled very hard with language, customs and life as a transplant. He married a Catholic and began to raise a family. Mary, his wife, took care of the religious matters, while he worked long hours for six to seven days a week.

Charlie got into *Genesis II* (the program we used then in Phase One) only to please his wife. Always honest, Charlie said what he thought, talked about his atheistic background and was accepted. At the end of the 18 sessions, each person in the group summed up what the experience meant for him or her personally. Charlie's statement was: "I was surprised I fit in with these people. They listened to me, and nobody laughed."

Charlie continued with the small group into the prayer module. Another year passed. Slowly, Charlie came to accept that God might be interested in him. Because of the regular meetings with the people of his small community and the faith-sharing environment, he had a chance to at least look at the possibility of God.

Charlie came into the big church through the little church. He is presently in the catechumenate, supported by his small community. A member of his SCC accompanies him to each RCIA evening.

Charlie probably would never have found his way into the church without the small group. At least that's the way Charlie and Mary see it.

CHAPTER FOUR

Pastoring the 'Pastors'

*T*he Small Church Community is really a church. Therefore, that church needs a pastor! The term carefully chosen at St. Elizabeth Seton to designate the pastoral leader of the small community is *pastoral facilitator*. The "PF" is often a couple, especially if the small community is mostly couples.

The word *facilitator* in this title refers to the PF's being at the service of the other members of the group, helping them relate to each other, keeping the group true to its purpose. The critical presumption is that the Holy Spirit speaks *in each person* in the small community and *through each person* for the others. Thus the small community's PF (like the parish's pastoral staff) need not necessarily be the wisest, holiest or most articulate.

The leader, in fact, works at not being the expert—the person everyone else addresses comments toward, the one giving approval. The facilitator is also *not* the problem-solver, *not* the counselor, *not* the teacher. Rather, the facilitator insures an environment where all members of the group can contribute to each other and where each person takes responsibility for the rest. The church always fails when only one person tries to take care of the community.

The very term *facilitate* means to bring out the best already present in people through a process of interaction. Thus the small community's leader facilitates communication.

The word *pastoral* refers primarily to tying this Small Church Community to the larger parish. Different members may take turns facilitating the group at times, but only one person or couple serves as the community's pastoral link to the parish.

The pastor of the Catholic Small Church Community does what the parish's canonical pastor or the bishop does: enable each person to bring his or her gifts to the entire group, help people in the church listen to each other, keep the vision of church before the members, connect this level of church to the other levels of church. (See the chart on page 14.)

A STORY

I am a teacher, and I've been a PF for less than two years. The hardest part is the underlying *don'ts: Don't* teach. *Don't* preach. *Don't* manipulate. I liken facilitating to steering a canoe. I went canoeing once and quickly discovered that if you turn too far in either direction, you hit a bank. I hit many banks until I learned that steering is a very gentle motion.

Facilitating works the same way. Our canoe is made up of the many years of Catholic teaching and experience that each member brings to our meetings. Each member of the group does his or her own paddling. Sometimes our discussions send us toward one bank or the other; sometimes one person in the canoe paddles too hard, sending us in a circle; or someone who hardly paddles at all can also cause us to circle. The facilitator's job is to gently steer, getting people back on the subject and giving everyone a chance to share thoughts and ideas. It is never the facilitator's job to take over the movement of the canoe with an outboard motor.

Unlike canoeing—which I never mastered—facilitating can be learned by anyone. All you have to do is trust God and pray. He will do the rest.

Keeping Pastoral Facilitators a Top Priority

Commitment, or lack of commitment, to the parish plan to restructure into Small Church Communities shows clearly in the amount of time and energy spent on pastoral facilitators.

Commitment to the church at any level demands that great care be given in providing that church community with a pastor. You will know that Small Church Communities are your parish's real goal when the selection, initial training and continuing formation of pastoral facilitators becomes the top priority of your parish *and* its staff.

Making pastoral facilitators a priority keeps the church at the smaller level a priority. And the further into the process you get, the more time and energy pastor and staff will have to devote to PFs to keep them in first place. Each new small community means another pastoral facilitator who needs initial training and continuing formation. For that reason, a parish should begin small communities a few at a time. It does no good to restructure a parish into Small Church Communities, if you can't train and support PFs for them.

How much staff time are we talking about? Initial training consists of six sessions. Ongoing support and formation involves monthly meetings for small groups of PFs with pastoral staff—plus an annual retreat. (The materials we developed at St. Elizabeth Seton for each of these settings are available from St. Anthony Messenger Press under the title: *Pastoring the 'Pastors': Resources for Training and Supporting Pastoral Facilitators for Small Faith Communities*.) In addition, some staff person needs to be available outside of these formal settings for one-on-one advice-giving.

Pastoral facilitators are pastoring the church *with* the pastor. Yet they develop slowly into the pastoring role. Some pastoral facilitators at St. Elizabeth Seton—even after several years and to my great consternation!—would still slip and call their small communities "prayer groups." Other PFs found faith-sharing difficult and were mostly silent at PF meetings for as long as a year. I was always disappointed when I found pastoral facilitators who were not taking time regularly for individual prayer and reflection. And some PFs who would get involved in other parish ministries would be puzzled at the staff's suggestion that they focus on pastoring as their sole church involvement.

For many months—usually over at least two years—the facilitators heard, but didn't completely appreciate the meaning of these words: "Your small group of people is really an expression of church" and "You really do pastor a Small Church Community." After all, few of us Catholics have ever experienced church at this basic level. Eventually, though, these new pastoral leaders do come to appreciate the pastoral plan of the parish and their role in that plan. Then all the effort by the staff—the continual repetition and reinforcement—pays off. But only by keeping the PFs a priority can they be brought to this point. The care and community the bishop ideally shares with his presbyterate is the model of care and community the pastor/pastoral staff shares with pastoral facilitators. In a large archdiocese with 1,000 priests, the bishop cannot relate personally to all the priests by being part of their ongoing small communities; but he must find some way to make his presence felt and to make his pastors a personal priority. Together, bishop and priests must share a vision and come to experience the bond they share. The same is true for the pastor and the parish's PFs. Words alone won't do it. If the pastor of the parish cannot personally be present for all the PF meetings, he must find other ways to convey his interest and support. *If the PFs do not see the pastors or the parish administrator regularly at their PF meetings, they can easily begin to see this Small Church Communities project as just one more parish program.*

The time and energy spent on PFs pays rich dividends for the church—as well as for the pastor and pastoral staff. My own pastoring and my own personal faith developed greatly through my association with PFs. Much of the regular meetings with the PFs after the first year simply involve being there for and with them, sharing one's own faith and sometimes lack of faith, and inviting these pastoral assistants to pray for and with the staff.

A Word to Priests

The reserves of energy and stamina that this pastoral plan calls for come to the pastor from the church community itself. The promise of restructuring is a promise of personal renewal for the pastoral staff for several reasons:

1) The pastor and staff are not alone in pastoring. They share in this with many pastoral facilitators of small

communities, and the commitment of PFs is motivating.
Gradually the PFs bring to the monthly meeting with the pastor
or the administrator how they experience the everyday faith of
Catholics, see real regard for fellow parishioners developing,
handle the frustration of hearing perpetual complaints, manage
those in the group with causes, as well as those who miss
frequently and participate poorly. One pastoral associate at St.
Elizabeth Seton made a very insightful remark after meeting
with pastoral facilitators for a year: "They really know how it
feels for us. I don't feel like I'm carrying the parish alone."

2) Having a direction worthy of one's best effort gives
energy. Much of present pastoral work is repetitive. But with
this pastoral plan we are moving somewhere, actually forming
the church in a significant way.

I experienced this kind of rejuvenation myself after almost
20 years of priesthood. When I once complained of my lack of
success in convincing parishioners to try small communities—
with only 25 percent of the parish participating after 10 years—
a member of the pastoral staff said, "At least you are failing at
the right things." And she was right!

I have found great reserves of energy over the years
because I now have a specific and clear direction against which
to measure success and failure. "Failing at the right thing" is
different than other kinds of parish failure, such as "spinning
one's wheels" or "burning out" with too much activity.

3) The sharing of one's life and experience of God in
everyday life is in itself reviving. Being trusted with the faith
stories of others at PF meetings also touches the pastoral
person's faith—or lack of faith.

The community of the church, then, becomes a great
source of strength for the priests and staff of the parish.
Restructuring allows the parish's pastoral person to be more a
part of the church and to receive strength as well as give
strength to others. Although many pastoral people won't find
this sense of belonging to the people of the church a new
experience, the depth, regularity and pastoral leadership of the
small communities are more life-giving to the pastor and the
staff than they probably expect at the outset.

Many, perhaps, most, of us priests, find it difficult to share
our own experience of faith and life with others: with other

priests or with laypeople. We don't just begin faith-sharing overnight, but grow gradually in our ability for this. Cursillo, different kinds of sharing retreats and various formats for small fraternities of priests meeting together regularly can help a priest in his ability to share. It helps to know that many of your fellow priests are involved in the same personal struggle to grow in sharing their lives with others and that we are all paying some of the price for the church to be reborn in this age.

What or who keeps you going and gives you energy?

Who knows you and your story both within and beyond the parish? Who could?

Who presently pastors with you? With whom could you share this work?

Selecting Pastoral Facilitators

Theoretically, pastoral facilitators could be formed before small communities are even begun in the parish. Then they could be assigned to groups as the groups start up. But we don't recommend this approach. Better to start first with the group and the beginning experience. Then, when the beginning experience is well along, train pastoral facilitators. The advantage to this approach is that facilitator training can draw upon a real group experience. The other advantage is that the pastoral facilitator is a real member of the group, learning and participating like everybody else.

When should a PF be formally identified for training? And *who* should be chosen—and *how*?

When. When to begin the pastoral facilitator training is not set in stone. There are real advantages to giving the group the initial experience *without* a designated pastoral leader. More people are likely to take responsibility for the life of the group. The *Come As You Are* program, for example, gives clear instructions so a group can easily rotate facilitation.

Of course, as mentioned earlier, it is important that, as each initial group is formed, some person—or couple—be included who at least appears to have the potential for eventually assuming the PF role. That person is asked to call the initial group together and facilitate the first session. He or she is also asked to call absent members, arrange for meetings in members' homes and to be the communication link to the parish.

Actual PF training, however, usually begins only after Phase One of a small group is well under way.

How. Different pastors and pastoral staffs will feel comfortable with various means of actually settling on pastoral facilitators. Some may allow the emerging small communities to select their own candidates for PF training; most, however, will want more of a direct hand in the selection.

Because the small group is on a long process in developing into a base church, the group's choice of a pastoral facilitator early on may not be the right pastor for the long haul. For example, the initial choice of the group might be the most outspoken and charming individual, who tends to dominate. And leaders, once chosen, are not easy to dispose of.

The reality is that the PFs will be in a special relationship with the parish's pastor and pastoral staff. These parish leaders are not present in each small church. The way they do influence and give direction to these small communities is through pastoral facilitators. The pastor and the staff share their pastoring responsibility with the PFs and must have confidence in them.

For this reason, pastoral facilitators should be chosen slowly and prayerfully with input from the staff and from the core team. Asking for specific time commitments of two or three years is very helpful so that there is a graceful opportunity for pastoral leadership to rotate if necessary. Most PFs, however, are still growing into their role after the first four or five years.

It would be better for a pastor and staff unfamiliar with parishioners to take several years to get to know people well before inviting people to share the pastoral role than to rush in and then have to live for years with poor selections. *The church deserves good pastors.* The church throughout history has always paid too great a price for the selection of inadequate pastors for every level of church. We don't want to replicate that pattern.

Who. What qualities make for good pastoral facilitators? The same qualities the church seeks in its pastors at every level of church. Here is a partial list of characteristics that would help a person or couple pastor well:

- a love and concern for the church at all levels
- the ability to make people feel comfortable and at ease
- a personal sense of God
- a good listener
- the ability to affirm others
- freedom from parish controversies; not hooked on particular issues
- responsibility and follow-through
- openness to change
- good self-esteem (Avoid like the plague the person who needs to be noticed, who grabs for attention, who appears unproductive in other areas of life and unhappy at home.)

The pastor/pastoral staff must be able to *work with* the PF—not necessarily *like* the PF. And the role has room for various personalities. As long as the PF has the qualities to facilitate a small community and can maintain enough of a trust level with the parish staff to share faith with that staff, that PF can work.

A S T O R Y

I am a 40-year-old accountant, married and the father of three children. I happen to like clear assets and debits, and I would be much more comfortable if the world was more black and white, like my profession.

I have been a pastoral facilitator for nearly three years. My wife chooses not to be a pastoral facilitator with me but she does come to the small community meetings.

I'm a Catholic who is uncomfortable being challenged all

the time, but I know this is the way Jesus meant it to be. The SCC is an opportunity to share my faith as an adult. My own doubts and fears are not unique, which gives me strength to keep trying to have a relationship with Jesus. Being a pastoral facilitator over three years has made me grow in faith and learn to trust God and others more. This kind of trust and reflection is definitely not the environment of my workplace, but I'm growing at my pace and in the way I can.

What parishioners would you identify right now as prospective pastoral facilitators? Why?

Formation of PFs

Once potential PFs are identified, they are asked for six evenings of their time to explain what these small groups in the parish can become and what continuing to be a leader will mean. The commitment is for the six sessions only. After the six sessions a person can either accept the pastoral role for a specified period of two or three years or not accept—no obligation.

The six training evenings help prospective PFs get to know each other, form initial bonds, experience reflective prayer and understand the church much better. If, after these six sessions, the prospects agree to become pastoral facilitators, then the new PFs spend an overnight retreat together. After this initial training, the PFs then have a regular monthly meeting together. Every year afterward, there is another overnight retreat. (Formats for training, retreats and monthly meetings can be found in the resource book *Pastoring the 'Pastors'* from St. Anthony Messenger Press.)

The same eight to 12 PFs who bond together in the initial six-session training continue together as a group of PFs for their own yearly retreat and their own monthly meeting. Thus, besides belonging to their Small Church Community, the PFs now belong to a small group of fellow PFs as well. They develop as a community with each other and with the pastors of the parish and, perhaps, with a designated staff person, as well. The number is kept small to allow for sharing. Without regular and consistent meetings, they can't become a real community.

PFs cannot develop as well by bringing all the PFs together to form a huge group for one evening each month. The large group may be more efficient in terms of staff time and effort, but the pastors need to be pastored—that is, to be heard well, to be noticed as individuals, to listen to each other. Obviously the busy pastor and pastoral staff will have to do the monthly formation of PFs within the time constraints of the parish, The final word, however, is that the church does not prosper at any level when we skimp on our pastors.

The monthly meeting is a priority commitment for the pastoral facilitator, even if it means canceling an SCC meeting to attend. This time each month is really the only ongoing reinforcement and formation they have.

The monthly PF meeting consists of two parts: (1) a modeling for the SCC meeting by sharing one's faith experience and praying together; (2) a practicum and discussion on each SCC, always keeping confidences. (Names and identities of people in the communities are always kept within the small community.)

The PFs are a genuine help to each other. They certainly develop a real bond with people doing the same ministry in the church, and they understand each other's frustrations and successes in pastoring. I do not believe the small community's pastoral leaders can last long without this community with other PFs. This is the main way to help leaders of the church grow in personal faith reflection, develop the pastoral qualities the church needs and stay aware of the larger church.

Summing Up

An executive, a homemaker, a mechanic—all can pastor small communities. So can single people or couples. (A couple who share the pastoring task usually grow closer to each other, as well as help each other assess the dynamics of the group.) A lot of different personalities can also pastor here, as in the larger church. But there is no getting lost in the crowd in leading a

Small Church Community.

It is more difficult in the smaller church to compensate for a leader's defects in sociability or communication skills. Over the years of meeting together at least monthly, the most surprising assortment of PFs can develop the art of pastoring and come to a great appreciation of the church at every level.

A STORY

I am 55 years old and the PF for an SCC with mostly younger couples. Through the SCC I found that my faith had to be shared in order for it to grow. By learning to share my beliefs, I have found that my beliefs are stronger and mean much more to me—not just the parts that I like and that are easy, but also those things that I dislike and that are hard.

We have all grown in our faith, and it is a joyful thing to watch people grow in faith and trust in God—to see the closeness that has grown among all of us.

The SCC I pastor has become an extension of my family. Because of our listening and sharing, we have all become more aware of our part in the whole church. We are all separate parts of the same body, the body of Christ. We are not just a group, or a collection of different people; we are bonded together to be the church.

A Caution

Because so much of the pastor's and of the staff's time and effort needs to be spent on training and supporting pastoral facilitators, some parishioners may falsely perceive them as a special "in group" of the parish. One part of the solution is for each PF to help his or her small community articulate often its identity as the church at a small level. The prominent and primary reality is the community; the pastoral person exists only to help that community develop.

What are the pastoral qualities God has given the pastor and staff of your parish—as individuals and as a staff?

What one or two pastoral qualities would you (they) need to develop?

What first step do you (they) need to take to develop this quality?

CHAPTER FIVE

Being Church for the Long Haul

The three stages in the development of the Small Church Community overlap, and there is no simple progression from one stage to the next. The experiences of each stage are reinforced continually and learned at a deeper level.

Phase Three: Owning the Church's Story

This third experience is essential at some point for a small group to become church at the smaller level. At this stage the group begins regularly to take the Sunday Gospel or other Sunday Scriptures as their point of reference in reflecting on their lives and sharing faith with one another. Other materials can also be used: other Scripture, sacramental rites, the Creed, encyclicals, Church history. The point is for the group to make the church's story a touchstone in their individual lives and in the life of their Small Church Community. The goal is to remain faithful to that experience of the church as we find it in the New Testament and over time.

The format for group gatherings in this third stage revolves around three or four key experiential questions that can help relate one's life to the church's story. (The reason for three or four questions rather than just one is to insure that each person can relate to at least one of the questions and has a choice.) These questions are meant to *focus* one's life in terms of the Gospel or the Tradition so that a person begins to experience the church in a personal way.

These "focus questions" are meant to be both experiential and personal—not factual, such as, "What is this Gospel saying?" or intellectual, such as, "What do you think about this Gospel?" Yet questions should be based upon the *objective meaning* of the text, not some metaphorical or purely subjective interpretation. (Each Sunday Gospel does have an objective meaning and was written deliberately to proclaim that meaning clearly. Reading a particular passage with a 20th-century mind-set can cloud that meaning, but a little commentary can help the average Catholic get at the church's story of faith.)

Good focus questions are also open-ended—that is, able to be answered on several different levels or in several different ways without steering a person to just one answer. They also draw on everyday experience, avoid religious jargon and never settle for a mere yes or no answer.

The chart on page 67 shows examples of focus questions developed for three Sunday Gospels.

This method of blending the objective truth of the church's story with one's own story is ascribed to Thomas H. Groome and called Shared Christian Praxis. (See chart on page 68.) Often referred to simply as Groome's process, it takes the church's experience in the form of Scripture, Tradition and Teaching as a focus for understanding one's own experience of life and God. Much of the process in the Adult Catechumenate follows this pattern, as does the modern approach to religious education. So does the modern homily.

Shared Christian Praxis helps us get beyond both the purely personal—"What does the Gospel say to *me*?"—and the merely factual—"Who wrote this passage and when?" Always there is the opportunity to reflect on one's experience and to listen to others' experience of life and faith.

The sharing makes the experience better and completes the experience. Hearing others' experiences in the group opens a person in new ways to the church's story. This process repeated over the years has great potential to enrich individual lives, the life of the Small Church Community and the life of the parish. The Gospels are no longer the same old familiar stories heard since childhood, stories of long ago, of wonders past. The

Sample Focus Questions

SCRIPTURE PASSAGES

FOCUS QUESTIONS

On the evening of that first day of the week when the doors were locked where the disciples were, for fear of the Jews, Jesus came and stood in their midst and said to them, "Peace be with you." When he had said this, he showed them his hands and his side. The disciples rejoiced when they saw the Lord. [Jesus] said to them again, "Peace be with you. As the Father has sent me, so I send you." And when he had said this, he breathed on them and said to them, "Receive the Holy Spirit. Whose sins you forgive are forgiven them, and whose sins you retain are retained." (John 20:19-23)

Name ways the peace of Christ becomes a recognizable gift in your life. What difference does it make? What difference would you like it to make?

What are some of the "locked doors"—or barriers—in your life? How can you change?

When the apostles returned, they explained to [Jesus] what they had done. He took them and withdrew in private to a town called Bethsaida. The crowds, meanwhile, learned of this and followed him. He received them and spoke to them about the kingdom of God, and he healed those who needed to be cured. As the day was drawing to a close, the Twelve approached him and said, "Dismiss the crowd so that they can go to the surrounding villages and farms and find lodging and provisions; for we are in a deserted place here." He said to them, "Give them some food yourselves." They replied, "Five loaves and two fish are all we have, unless we ourselves go and buy food for all these people." Now the men there numbered about five thousand. Then he said to his disciples, "Have them sit down in groups of [about] 50." They did so and made them all sit down. Then taking the five loaves and the two fish, and looking up to heaven, he said the blessing over them, broke them, and gave them to the disciples to set before the crowd. They all ate and were satisfied. And when the leftover fragments were picked up, they filled 12 wicker baskets. (Luke 9:10-17)

Whom has God put into your life to feed?

How has God fed you over the last year? The last month?

What in you is still incomplete in a way that only God can fill?

What are the hungers of our world? How do these affect you?

Shared Christian Praxis

PRAXIS:
- Means "reflection on life."
- Means learning by doing and learning from what we are doing.
- It is reflection and action combined.
- Praxis is a way of learning that begins by inviting people to reflect upon their own life experiences.

CHRISTIAN:
- To come to know God in Jesus Christ.
- We need to hear the Christian story over and over.
- Christian story: the whole tradition of our Catholic Christian faith.
- We need to hear the story as a focus when we reflect on the present activity of God in our experiences.

SHARED:
- Dialogue takes place with God; prayer is an explicit part of the process.
- Dialogue takes place with one another; each member is invited to express his or her personal reflections and hear those of others.
- *Dialogue* here means *sharing our faith together* in the light of the Christian story.
- We make faith our own so as to come to a *response* of lived faith.

Scriptures begin to strike a chord in us because they speak to our own experience.

If done well, with good focus questions, this process allows anyone the chance to reflect on and communicate faith and life. Education level and social class need not become determining factors as to who can or cannot contribute to the sharing.

The process works! Slowly but surely people get used to the pattern and their discernment skills develop. Most of us were not taught religion by this experiential approach. This process, however, does open us Catholics to the Lord in our lives *and* connect our individual lives to the Lord experienced in the Catholic community's life through Scripture or Tradition.

And this process can keep us growing as Catholics indefinitely! The materials don't run out; the book doesn't end. Shared Christian Praxis gives the small church an ongoing way to connect life and faith without having to search continually for new and better programs.

Getting Good Focus Questions

A particular Sunday reading can often be a "pain" to the homilist. But sometimes the obscure or difficult passage turns out to be the best for the small group. It all depends on having good focus questions. How are these questions developed?

At our parish we began with one staff person printing a small commentary on the coming Sunday's Gospel with two to three questions focusing on lived experience in terms of the Gospel. These could then be used by all Phase Three groups in the parish. Or a few people on the staff or core team could develop the questions. There are several good resources listed in Appendix A. (See the guidelines for creating and using good focus questions on pages 70-71.)

Guidelines for Creating Good Focus Questions

1. Pray over the Scripture passage before beginning to develop questions. Leave time for the Spirit to work.

2. Keep questions open-ended. Avoid questions
   - that can be answered yes or no
   - that have a predetermined answer
   - that have a right or wrong answer.

3. Stay away from questions of fact. ("What does it mean...?" is a question of fact.) Focus on recalling the life experiences of group members.

4. Keep questions short and simple.

5. Avoid religious jargon and churchy phrases.

6. Stay away from superlatives (for example, most, significant, overwhelming) and absolutes (for example, nothing, everything). This kind of language can make participants feel that their own experiences are too ordinary to talk about.

7. Prepare more than one question. Some people will find the second or third question speaks to them in a way the first question doesn't. This allows for everyone to share.

8. Use good starters for questions:
   "Relate an experience" or "Describe an experience" is better than the authoritative "Tell us about."
   "From your personal experience" is a good way to begin.

9. Be on guard against these bad starters for questions:
   "Do you" always deadends in yes or no.
   "What does it mean" signals a questions of fact.

Guidelines for Using Focus Questions

1. Give the group time to reflect on the questions privately before sharing.

2. Create an atmosphere in which people feel free to share on whatever level they wish.

3. Break up into groups of three or four for discussion.

4. Always make sure there is an opportunity to discuss more than just one focus question. This insures that the greatest number of people will contribute to the interchange.

5. Be sure to follow up the small-group discussion of focus questions with large-group exchange. Ask the large group to consider questions such as these:
   - What further insights am I aware of as a result of the listening in the group of three to four?
   - How have I grown as a result of my sharing?
   - Especially the question: So what difference will this make when I go home to my family? To my workplace? To the way I vote? In my concern for the poor?

6. Remind participants never to relate another participant's contribution from the small group in the large-group sharing.

7. Encourage individuals to keep reflecting on the focus questions after the meeting.

The PFs might compose the focus questions. After composing the questions, PFs could choose at least two, take 10 minutes of silent reflection, break into groups of three, share and then return to the large group to share the further insights or resolutions that arose in the small group and pray together. This would take no more than half the monthly PF meeting.

The focus questions on page 67 were composed at a monthly meeting by three-year veteran pastoral facilitators. Note the open-endedness and depth of these questions. They are simple enough—relating experiences from everyday life so easily overlooked.

A fine source for both staff and PFs in creating focus questions is *Breaking Open the Word of God*, by Karen Hinman (Paulist Press). Another very helpful source for focus questions is *Serendipity New Testament for Groups* (Serendipity House).

Focus questions for the three-year liturgical cycle, composed by 7,500 people, mostly in North America, but with a good representation from around the world, appear in *Faith Sharing for Small Church Communities: Questions and Commentaries on the Sunday Readings*, available from St. Anthony Messenger Press. A Spanish edition is also available.

Focus questions by pastoral facilitators were often clearer and touched life experience better than the focus questions composed by the staff. I remember one example in particular regarding the Third Sunday of Lent in Cycle C. The Gospel was the story of the barren fig tree (Luke 13:6-9). The owner tells the worker to tend and fertilize the tree another year; perhaps it will bear fruit. This very simple open-ended focus question emerged from the group of PFs: "Recall a second-chance experience God gave you." People can stay with that question for a long time and go many directions with their responses: second chances with relationships; with repenting a moral failure; with appreciating one's life, marriage, middle age and so on. Who cannot find second chances throughout a lifetime? But then to connect our second-chance experiences with this Gospel story and with the way the church continues to discover God working today—profound!

One's own life and the riches of the church's life keep reinforcing each other. Twentieth-century Americans by and large do not live at this level—and are losing their hearts and souls because of it. How atypical, yet hopeful, for ordinary, busy people to ask good questions about their lives—and to keep asking them!

Now let us return to our original question about who generates focus questions for the base churches. I suppose that eventually the Small Church Community could compose questions true to the church's story for itself. We never got that far in our parish, however; only the PFs and the staff did the composing. But if involving PFs only complicates the plan for your parish, then assign the task to a staff person.

Who supplies the focus questions is not the most important point. Getting good questions by whatever means is the key—and will remain the key—to the ongoing life of Small Church Communities living out their call to be church together.

Getting Even Smaller

The kind of faith sharing which characterizes Phase Three happens best in groups of three or four—not the eight to 12 of the base church. Therefore the small church will have to divide up into two or three even smaller groups for this part of the gathering. (Counting off at each session assures a good mix of people.)

People will say things in these smaller groupings that they won't say in the larger group and, in general, the sharing will be at a deeper level. Also, people who tend to keep silent in a large group will speak more readily in a group of three or four. And those who tend to say too much or react too quickly in a larger group will find it easier to make sure that everyone has a chance to speak in this smaller setting.

Dynamics are simply different in a smaller group. Not to divide up into these smaller groupings of three or four is to miss great potential for a deeper sharing of faith. It is important to insist on this as part of the ongoing life of the base church. (Groups who have used *Come As You Are* and *Praying Alone and Together* as their first and second programs will already have experienced this smaller group exchange as a regular part of their meetings.)

Naming the Experience, Evaluating the Progress

After the small community has been praying together and connecting their personal stories with the church's story for several months, members should start to articulate that this small group is the church at another level. Members *often have* to hear themselves say why they are meeting together: *not simply* for spiritual enrichment or personal support, *but also* to bring about the church.

This gathering of eight to 12 people is not simply a prayer group or a Scripture-sharing, therapy or support group. This small community is "the church in miniature."

Each member would do well to read this book, *Creating Small Church Communities*, but only as the group has become quite comfortable in the third phase. While sharing with good focus questions on the Sunday Scripture comes first, discussing this book, chapter by chapter, can help everyone in the small community better appreciate the vision of the church. Another very good resource to help the SCC member appreciate the larger vision of church is the video *20/20 Vision For the Parish*, with its study guide.

People make a different kind of commitment to a small community they perceive as church and not just a group of people they enjoy or even connect faith with. And the way the group needs to evaluate itself is to ask how well the church is being realized in their midst.

A contract between group members early on can facilitate such evaluation by clarifying individual and group expectations. (A sample contract is given in Appendix B.) The agreement includes points such as listening and respecting each other in the group, being honest, making the meetings and staying true to the group's purpose.

The evaluation of the small community by its members— done periodically and with the freedom to be honest—is a real safeguard to the community's future. Because small communities are close, negative criticism can be extremely difficult. Regular evaluations are a help because the very regularity says that the evaluation is ongoing and needed—not just a result of a problem. Formats for evaluating the Small Church Community by members are included in Appendix C.

The PFs already have a model for such evaluation because they are asked to evaluate their monthly meetings on a regular basis also.

The Two-Hour Format for the Small Church Community

The heart of the Small Church Community is connecting one's own life story with the church's story and sharing that connection with the other members. The focus questions from Scripture or Tradition are the means.

Another presupposition is that each member is taking personal time between meetings to be reflective and to pray for each other as well as for themselves. Providing time at the beginning of the SCC meeting for members to pair off and review their lives is a way for people to be accountable for living a faith life. (While the review of life can be quite helpful, many SCCs choose not to use it.) See Appendix D for a simple three-part format for the review of one's life with another person. This can be photocopied for each member. The review of life asks questions about prayer and action and presumes a good bit of trust among its members.

Some SCCs choose to print the review of life on a card for each person which all the other members sign. This could be a two- or three-fold card that could be carried in one's wallet or purse.

One part of the SCC format is called "Appreciating the Vision." This facet of the format includes input and discussion about how our particular SCC fits with the other parish SCCs, along with consideration of the total vision of parish. Here members may look at why the entire parish is structuring all its programs, activities and committees so that people are always reflecting about life and helping each other connect their everyday lives and faith, and at ways the SCC is countercultural to the larger society. "Appreciating the Vision" may not take place at every meeting and cannot take over the life/faith reflection and prayer. But this appreciation of the larger vision does need to be a part of the SCC. Appendix A on page 101 suggests some resources under the heading "Resources for the

Vision of Restructuring the Parish."

The next section deals with service. The one-and-a-half- to two-hour meeting, then, would take over this format:

I. GATHERING, RELAXING, SETTLING IN
A. "How's your day/week?" in a word or one sentence.
B. Sometimes, an opening song.
C. Or, a few minutes of unstructured getting caught up with each other.

II. REVIEW OF LIFE (10 minutes)
A. Done in pairs.

III. LIFE/FAITH CONNECTION (50 to 70 minutes)
A. Personal quiet reflection (10 minutes)
1. Hearing the Scripture, especially the Gospel, of the upcoming Sunday (or some other Scripture, or something from the Tradition).
2. Each member is given a copy of the Scripture reading, a short commentary, and three or four focus questions.
B. Small groups of three to four (20 to 30 minutes)
1. Gather groups in different parts of the house.
2. Counting off can be a useful way of mixing people.
C. Entire group sharing (20 to 30 minutes)
1. Further reflections together, but speaking only to one's own experience and not to what another said in the small group of three to four.
2. The "so what?" question: What difference will this make when I go home to my family, my work place, the neighborhood, the way I relate to the poor, the way I vote?

IV. SHARED PRAYER (15 to 25 minutes)
A. Many different forms from the long Tradition are possible. See *Praying Alone and Together* listed in Appendix A.

V. APPRECIATION OF THE VISION
A. May be occasional.
B. Appendix A, under Resources for the Vision of

Restructuring the Parish, can be helpful.

VI. EVALUATION OF THE MEETING (10 minutes)
A. This often happens informally by way of conversation.
B. Every so often, a more formal process should be used. Appendices B, C and E can be useful in helping look at the interaction between members.

VII. REFRESHMENTS AND SOCIAL AT THE END

Hand-Holding or Out-Reaching

Being "the church in miniature" means more than just connecting one's life experience with faith and praying with others in your small group while being linked pastorally to the larger parish. Being a Small Church Community means *service* both to the larger church community and to the world. Justice and peace commitments are not just add-ons to the church but constitutive—that is, essential—to the church at every level. Without service the church is not the church.

Service beyond the base church, however, usually comes in Phase Three, *after* the bonding of members within the group and the beginning of prayer and faith sharing. Thus a Small Church Community usually blossoms into service as it moves into Phase Three in the process of becoming a real church. Service, then, expresses the relationship with God and with the church that members of the small group are increasingly articulating for themselves and each other. Christian service in a small community is not second in importance, only second in timing.

Another reason for this placing service last in the process of becoming church is to counter the reality that most Americans find doing something easier than being together. "Keep busy" and "Stay productive" are the mottoes of our society. We Catholics can get so caught up in activities and causes that the experience of the Lord in our midst is often missed. No cause—even justice and peace—can substitute for a relationship with God and for relationships with others in the community of faith. The church at every level is founded by a Person and for a Person. Historically, whenever the church has given more attention to a particular ideology than to the Person of the Lord, the church has paid a great price. Christian service is most definitely what we must all be about, but service *as an expression* of our relationship with God and his people, not *as a substitute for* it.

The glue of the SCC is the basic human bonding that people experience with each other. They also need to look outward toward the world.

The small church community has two structures built in that will help it look outward beyond itself. The first structure is the Review of Life which asks the questions, "How is my attitude changing toward the most forgotten of our society?" and "What will I do?" (See Appendix D.) The other SCC structure is the sharing of the entire group immediately after the small groups of three to four. The "So-what" question is asked. "What difference will all this make when I go home to my family, my work place, the neighborhood, the way I relate to the poor, the way I vote?".

Besides, the Scriptures themselves are the focus of the SCC and constantly bring up the preferential love for the outcast.

How can an individual SCC look at real social change, at changing the structures that keep people poor? The best way is to be part of a parish that is doing this.

That parish can provide formation and invitation to its SCCs to participate in the particular efforts sponsored by the parish. More effective still is the larger interfaith, broad-based community organizing. It sytematically links diverse people together to cooperate on issues that can make a difference in an area. SCCs, then, can plug into an existing network of people working together to make good societal change happen.

Ordinary Life and Everyday Care

Sometimes it is easier to love humankind than the particular people we are with. Yet from the 34 Small Basic Christian Communities at St. Elizabeth Seton there are hundreds of stories of how people learned to love and care about other particular people right here and now.

I am impressed especially by the stories of quiet people, so often unnoticed in a parish, who did get noticed and appreciated in a smaller Church Community. One very low-key couple leaving for Atlanta because of a job transfer were genuinely pained by the move for two reasons: leaving the wife's mother *and* leaving their Small Church Community. Another very shy couple transplanted from Chicago, where all their roots had been sunk, eventually came to call this new place—not Chicago—home because of the eight others in their SCC. These often-missed and seldom-noticed deserve a place in the church.

One harried, overworked Chrysler engineer said, "My wife dragged me into this kicking and screaming. I told her, 12 sessions and that's it. I've only missed two times in five years. When she can't go, I go without her." Underneath the words and the testimonies is the reality of genuine care—and care by the church. Such care does not mean support without challenge. But the bottom line is this: Being loved and being irreplaceable to eight to 12 other people helps a person face the challenge to grow and find the courage to change. No admonitions or sermons are needed, just each person's willingness to say how it is really going and, finally, to pray about it in some fashion.

People in the group say what the priest might preach in the homily, but the people are speaking the church's faith from their own experience. One ordinary example comes from a 35-year-old man in a second marriage who had been sporadic about Mass on Sunday because of lack of motivation. I heard him say to his small community that he decided to attend the parish Mass the previous Sunday (after his initial decision not to) because he recalled comments from the last two group meetings. People had said that just as being there is important to the small community, so somehow that gets translated into being there for the larger community as well.

All the homilies about the church community needing every member for the Eucharist to be complete did not communicate what the Small Church Community said to that man—and he was doing the talking!

People speaking from experience and connecting that with

the basic truths of why we are Catholic or Christian—that's the
ordinary life of the small church. Out of this ordinary life grow
many extraordinary stories of care.

One small community, for example, invited an introverted
bachelor of 37, struggling with cancer, to join. His last 18
months were spent with this small church around him, even at
the hospital, and he died well. Where would Catholics like
Richard have found us, or where would we have found a loner
such as Richard except by being the church at this basic level?

Some people—probably most people—get lost in the big
church. So does too much living and dying. Our stories never
get told and, after a while, we forget to notice our own
experience. So much is so ordinary—so seemingly insignificant.
But then the church's own faith story gets lost for many and
begins to seem like mere theory and abstract philosophy. Thank
God an alternative exists!

Large Church/Small Church

Striking a balance between what is best done in and by the
Small Church Community and what is best done by the larger
church remains a continuing tension for a parish which
restructures. At St. Elizabeth Seton, for example, a parish
council member suggested that small communities welcome
new parishioners. Sounds great!

New people should receive a personal welcome by the
parish.

But there is a problem in attempting to co-opt the parish's
small communities for an ulterior purpose, albeit a good
purpose. These small churches are authentic churches and have
a life of their own that must be respected. The parish can
present its needs or objectives as possible services a particular
Small Church Community could assume. The choice, however,
is the small church's and not the parish's to impose.

A parish is not a branch office of the diocese but a
different level of church with a separate, though very
interdependent, existence. Just as no diocese would write the
detailed Christian service program for a parish, no parish
should attempt to do so for its base churches. Service will

emerge from the small community itself.

Please understand: The larger parish benefits immensely, actually is transformed, by the small communities. People do understand that the care received in a small parish group is the care of the parish and the church. As they experience the parish caring about them, they come to care about the parish and realize the responsibility to give something back. After the first two years of operative small communities, our parish was never short of people coming forward for any parish ministry. We always had catechists, parish council and commission people, and so on. People in small groups simply become more aware of other people and look beneath the "sea of humanity" at the Sunday Eucharist and elsewhere in life.

The following short statement from an independent, self-made man of 30, working six days a week, teaching drafting one to two evenings a week and working on a master's degree speaks volumes: During his second year in a Small Church Community he said: "I trust people more." This fine and talented man has great potential for the larger church, but only a smaller church will bring him to use his talents for the service of others.

Don't these small communities become cliquish, elitist, superior and divisive? True, people do develop a special bond with each other in a base church. This is the goal: for members to become close and invest in each other. But there is no more danger of exclusivity here than there is in the church at every level. Take, for example, the many parishes that confine almost all their resources within the parish community itself.

The main corrective to any tendency to exclusivity is the pastoral person who connects the church at one level to the next level of church. In the base church, it is the pastoral facilitator who keeps the mission of the larger church before the group. Sometimes the PF will need to push them to come up with ways not to appear cliquish—for example, not sitting together as a group during parish socials but reaching out to other parishioners. And, as we saw earlier in this chapter, one dynamic operating within the small church is that members are gradually opened to service beyond the small group as they become more comfortable with their identity as church.

One way to keep the Small Church Communities from

becoming cliques may be to change members or to mix and match groups. But the reality is that a small community needs many years to develop. Groups go through stages of development and each group has a personality of its own. So base churches should not be reshuffled according to some preordained timetable.

As more parishes begin to restructure into small communities, we will have to draw upon that collective experience to address more adequately the right timetable for changing groups. Then we will write another book!

A STORY

I have been active in church work for the past 20 years. I taught in the Catholic school and later was Director of Religious Education in the same parish. I was in this position during the Vatican II changes and struggled like all other Catholics to understand what was happening. Because of my position I was fortunate to have many opportunities to help me in my search.

It became clear to me that the experience of church in large parishes was lacking something. I felt I needed to meet with other Catholics to search out how God works (or doesn't work) in our lives. I needed to have others' help in that search. I recruited two other DREs and a couple of secretaries, and we began meeting once a week before work to share our faith. This went on for two years.

But this experience had one negative effect on me: I felt separated from the rest of the parishioners. I was reflective—they, on the whole, were not. My group developed a sense of belonging, but not with the church members. It became *they* and *I*. (I suppose charismatics, Marriage Encounter groups, and so on probably feel the same.)

I am now a member of St. Elizabeth Seton parish and a member of a Small Church Community. The activity of the SCCs is basically the same as the group I met with previously. We share our faith in order to help each other find and appreciate how God works in our lives. The difference is that the SCCs have a tie to the parish through the pastoral facilitators, and the focus of the parish is to restructure the parish into Small Church Communities. It's no longer a feeling of *them* and *me*. It's a sense of oneness—of belonging. When I come to celebrate liturgy, I feel a oneness with the rest of the community. Not everyone is in a small community, but that doesn't matter. Through the SCCs I have become one with all in Christ.

To what level of the church do you personally experience the greatest belonging?

If you are a pastoral leader, how well do you connect your level of church to the next larger level? What would help you do this connecting better?

As a parishioner, to what degree does the care and trust you experience through church translate into the rest of your relationships? Into concern for the poor?

Why Some Communities Disband

Groups go through various stages and reach various plateaus. Commitment is needed to persevere together over time and stay true to purpose. More than one group at our parish seemed to fall into a period of dry routine, only to go on to a rebirth with a renewed sense of identity as church. So how long should a small community stay together?

Groups certainly need several years together to develop into base churches. Some may stay together indefinitely. The purpose is not to be always interesting to each other, not to provide new insights, and not to be best friends. The goal is to be a community of everyday disciples together. That means doing something for the church, not only for one's personal growth. Expectations of the group and of individuals have to be kept in line with that basic purpose.

Some small communities will come to a point where members see that the time has come to be a small church with others. The decision is as good as the reasons, and each group has to make that discernment.

Our little churches did, at times, lose members and even cease to exist as a grouping for various reasons—the pull of other activities on the members, the format of the meetings, lack of clarity on being the church and the reason for meeting together, personality conflicts, strong individual needs subverting the purpose of the group, poor bonding of members in the first year.

There are always individuals in parishes who seek out groups from a strong personal need. Their individual or family problems are so intense that they can absorb the group's whole attention and group members can get caught in giving advice or in taking on the problems personally. On the other hand, another personality type has a need to parent other adults and to have others be dependent. (This type should never be asked to be PF.) The purpose of the small church can be sidetracked by either personality type left unchecked. This is not a therapy group.

The best remedy to control the dominator or the person working out strong personal needs is for the small group (after it has been together for a while) to assess itself by regularly using: the points of the initial agreement (Appendix B), a regular group evaluation (Appendix C) and the Stages of Group Development (Appendix E). Appendix E describes stages a group goes through—necessary stages for growth. It also has helpful responses for each stage. The SCC would do well to look at and use this Appendix E on occasion.

Another reason must also be kept in mind: Reflection on life, prayer and sharing faith confront each individual with opportunities for value clarification and challenges for personal growth. Change from a familiar and comfortable life-style is not easy for people—and a small church can be the source of constant challenge. The big church of the parish provides a better hiding place—and some people will choose to retreat to that bigger church. There is no way to keep people in a group if they choose to leave. There are, however, some safeguards to keep a group together. One essential is to have an initial program that gets people to bond. If a member or couple misses often during the first 10 to 12 sessions, the belonging never is experienced and the group never develops well. After attempts to reach out to a missing member by personal visits and by phone, the absentee eventually must be confronted and pushed into a choice: to leave or to commit to attend.

Group members usually drop out by gradually slipping away. The reason given is that other commitments came up, or that one is now too busy. Those reasons are often just excuses; the real explanation is deeper and may have been brewing for a long time. The PF, if he or she is perceptive, tries to notice and address members who are quiet or uninvolved. Sometimes a PF might meet with a person individually to try to help deal with a festering issue.

To sum up the basics: Each Small Church Community is different. All go through stages. They must regularly evaluate themselves. Each group needs many years to develop. Don't disband too quickly.

CHAPTER SIX

The Other 75 Percent

*A*fter 10 years of dogged effort, St. Elizabeth Seton had just under 25 percent of all parishioners in Small Church Communities. Where does the parish find the time in all this restructuring for the other 75 percent not in small communities? Or the other 80 percent? Or the other 90 percent? These other parishioners—whatever their exact percentage—may be the majority for another generation or for much longer. We cannot give them the impression of being second-class Catholics.

The most important point to be emphasized about parish programming is the advisability of having all parish activities and committees include a little quiet time with one or more life reflection questions, in small groups of two or three.

A Balancing Act

The parish obviously doesn't just stop while restructuring goes on. The pastoral staff must also attend to sacramental preparation, Sunday liturgies, weddings, funerals, baptisms, Christian service, outreach, justice and peace programs, CCD, RCIA, parish council and commissions, festivals, building projects, cash flow. Can the parish at large be maintained and restructuring proceed at the same time?

Yes and no. Yes, there is a way to restructure and at the same time maintain the parish and take care of everybody at some level. No, we can't restructure the parish and continue doing everything else in exactly the same way as before. Every parish is already a balancing act where a great array of parishioner priorities, staff priorities and pastor priorities get juggled more or less successfully. A parish that decides to restructure according to this pastoral plan must now find a new balance—that is, its own best means to dropping, changing and amalgamating existing programs as it decides how quickly to proceed in restructuring. The following observations may help in your balancing act:

1) If one is committed to the pastoral plan for restructuring the parish, one will find a way!

2) Restructuring the parish is not easy. Know that we are speaking about an endeavor that takes years and decades. After the initial spurt of motivated parishioners, the second and third waves of response are slower and smaller. Some people wait for years to join; some groups, begun with enthusiasm, plateau after awhile and seem in trouble. Each small community actually goes through its own stages at its own pace and develops its own personality. One grand scheme or timetable can't be laid out and then efficiently executed.

3) Acting prematurely is irresponsible. Only slow and methodical planning will have lasting results. A realistic timetable is important. Start with yourself, the parish staff, the pastor. Go through the actual group experiences together. If the pastor can't build a little community of faith with his staff because the staff will not try, the pastor must begin to find new staff persons who are willing to be the church with him. No planner should attempt restructuring alone.

4) The parish staff needs to find some comfortable way to prevent the day-to-day business of the parish from stealing time from praying and sharing faith together as a staff. *Faith Sharing for Small Church Communities* has questions that a staff could use. Breaking into small groups of three would help.

5) The pastoral staff needs to focus continually on the parish plan during staff meetings. At each meeting the agenda might begin with restating the actual goal and then evaluating progress. Another approach is for the staff to assess consistently each parish activity in terms of its relation to the pastoral plan of restructuring. Staff members slowly develop an awareness of

how they will, indeed, be working differently in their own area of ministry, so that every parish program includes some kind of quiet reflection with life experience questions and an exchange in groups of two or three. The staff meeting is the place to keep reinforcing for each other where the parish is headed. Staff members can help each other develop experience questions that are appropriate to each parish program—questions that don't embarrass people. For example, the questions and process for bingo will need to be different than for the pastoral council.

The parish's staff can best affect the church and the little churches by being church with other pastoral leaders. One's pastoral style may be more private, individual and directive, but the church needs a modification of that style. The parishioner or parish leader is asked to keep developing a reflective life-style by listening to God in his or her own life and feelings. One may have a personality and style that moves from one activity to another, never staying on one course for long. The church needs a modification of that style too. A possible way to get consistency on a staff is to ask a strong goal-oriented person to keep bringing the staff back to the chosen pastoral plan of restructuring.

An Investment in the Future

The effects of base churches on the entire parish are far-reaching and long-lasting because the church itself is being constantly formed. Unlike renewal programs built on a charismatic personality or the particular priorities of an individual pastor or staff person, Small Church Communities continue even when key staff people leave or are transferred. So do formed and committed pastoral facilitators.

This does not happen without making an investment for the sake of this future. An investment entails going without today for the sake of tomorrow. The allocation of energy and time for the sake of base churches often means borrowing from the parish today for what will come back to our people many times over in the future. Even the 75 percent not in small communities will benefit more permanently and deeply in the near future because of the restructuring of the parish. Waiting until every immediate parish need is taken care of adequately will mean never investing in any future.

Some parish activities may have to go. Many of us simply cannot continue our present hectic pace and begin restructuring the parish, as well. Sometimes essential parish services can be covered by additional staff, sometimes by parishioners trained for a parish ministry. Sometimes, however, we simply may have to let go of some necessary parish activities and do other programs less than perfectly—at least for awhile.

Here's an example of what I mean: A program demanding a lot of energy and time in every parish today is the catechumenate. Now the catechumenate has a good number of roles to be filled: parish sponsors, personal sponsors, catechists and so on. The entire RCIA process is very important, of course, and has great potential for the parishioners taking on the various roles, for the inquirers/catechumens/elect and for the parish itself. But preparing people for these roles and involving the community take time and effort on the part of the staff, keep many people—usually promising leaders—from being in small communities, and may deprive the parish of pastoral facilitators.

Now weigh that against these points: (1) Small Church Communities, eventually, may have more of a direct role as a sponsor for catechumens. (2) These small communities provide an ongoing faith formation and an experience of the church for the whole parish. (3) Small Church Communities will produce fresh leaders for the RCIA as well as every other ministry—not just the same people doing the same jobs year after year. (4) The restructured parish gives the new Catholic who enters the church through RCIA a community to belong to and to share faith with long after Easter and Pentecost.

So, for awhile, some parishes may judge that the catechumenate may have to be trimmed down for the sake of restructuring the entire parish. This investment in the future will pay off because, in the end, the purpose of the RCIA will be better achieved.

Some other parish activities simply should be let go: particularly those that use valuable parishioner time in "doism"—for example, the rummage sale that eats up countless hours for a few hundred dollars without bringing parishioners together to share life or grow in faith.

Too many activities relativize every activity. When there are 15 activities in the parish each week and the parish bulletin is littered with announcements trying to attract the same active people (national statistics reveal that only 13 percent of Catholics are involved in the parish beyond weekend liturgy), Small Church Communities seem to become just one more program.

The Discipline of Priorities

A most critical pastoral act of love for the church may well be the discipline of priorities: back to basics, back to our heart and soul as a people. Priorities often involve painful choices between good activities and between good people. Letting go of genuinely helpful and caring programs can be difficult for people to understand. Some resulting wounds perhaps won't be healed in this world.

Just because an activity is for a good purpose does not necessarily justify keeping it. Nor is more activity better. Many Americans lead overstretched, hyperactive lives with little reflection. Calling people to more activity through the parish may not be a service at all.

The discipline of priorities doggedly keeps asking the same questions: Why do we exist? What are we trying to become? What comes first to get there? How does each present activity/project/expenditure contribute?

In the final analysis a decision must be made: Do we continue with the present structure of the parish and do lots of good programs and outreach for the masses of parishioners, or restructure the parish into smaller ongoing communities that are the church at a small level while maintaining the parish community.

Both are good alternatives and the community of faith grows both ways. In the present parish structure, many creative and traditional approaches and activities touch people. Even small groups are possible within the parish as now structured. But to make restructuring the goal of the parish is a different—

and a difficult—decision.

List every activity of any kind now going on in your parish.
Which of these activities could be simplified or dropped in order to
make time for this plan to succeed?

Check your list of key people. What parish activities would these
key people have to drop to make this restructuring plan work?
How can your parish discipline itself to keep its priorities?

The original question—how to restructure the parish into
small communities and continue to do all the other activities—
hasn't been answered. The other 75 percent of the people are
still there. There is no real definitive answer. This chapter posed
many considerations:

- Start the parish plan slowly. Decide among present
  activities those that need
  a) to be done less thoroughly
  b) to be delayed
  c) to be dropped for the sake of Small Church
     Communities.
- Assess, and possibly change, the expectations you place
  on yourself as the pastoral person.
- Stay the course of restructuring. Let that be a focus for
  all your other pastoring activities.
- Find people to share the vision and to work with you.

The real answer comes from you, the parishioner, staff or
pastor of the parish. Whether you do the pastoring individually
or as a pastoral staff, you provide the only possible answer
about how to take care of the other 75 percent of the parish not
in Small Church Communities. You must seek the answer in
your own parish situation.

The answer about what present activities should be
modified, dropped or combined usually will evolve slowly as
you put each step of the parish restructuring plan into action.
The answers come as you proceed. Please proceed!

A STORY

I have served for seven years as pastor of a parish that is 75 years old and made up of 1,800 households. We have a lot of senior citizens, but a good number of young families also. We operate an elementary school and religious education program. There is a fine parish council, with its commissions, as well as numerous active groups in the parish.

To say that this parish is "active" is an understatement. In the last year, we have celebrated 56 funerals, 51 weddings, 125 baptisms. We make 35 home Communion visits per week. There is a nursing home that the parish is responsible for, as well as a very active St. Vincent de Paul Society. Every fall the parish has a festival, which serves to bring the whole community together.

Our staff consists of 30 full-time and part-time employees, including the grade school faculty. A pastoral staff of six members joins with me in coordinating and working directly with all the parish ministries and activities. Parishioners are involved as much as possible, which means many committee and group meetings, which take up a major portion of the staff's time.

The pastoral philosophy from which I operate is that the priest "rubs elbows with the people" and tries to be involved in their lives. He works with them, providing encouragement and direction. Priests, and staff, ought to be present when the "folks" are around; the pastoral ministry is not simply fulfilling tasks. A style of ministry based on "presence" obviously takes personal time and energy.

The bad news is that next summer our parish will most probably have only one full-time priest serving it. In previous years it had three priests; it has been served by two priests since the early 70's.

I find the concept of small basic communities very attractive and desirable. The problem I face is how to be dedicated to this concept and do everything else necessary in a large parish community that is already established. When I first read this book, the thought of a total restructuring of this parish was almost oppressive—a feeling not unlike that of a beginning swimmer looking at the English Channel.

After careful thought I have come to realize that much of

this frustration comes from focusing on the end result—the final step of the plan—instead of starting where we are at present. One of the most important elements of the small basic community concept is to devise a plan—a step-by-step plan (including time periods) spelling out how this parish community will move toward the desired goal of restructuring. Once a plan is determined, you only set your expectations according to the step called for at that time. This approach makes the whole concept more realistic, and more possible.

In my own situation I am thinking of two practical steps that we can take to begin the process. My expectation at present is that I will probably be here as pastor for two to three more years. During that time I will plan, first, to share this book and the small basic community concept with the parish staff and discuss its implications for us. Second, I will suggest that we find as many ways as possible for existing parish groups to share faith and prayer together. From Communion calls to council meetings, we will seek opportunities to bring this experience to members of our community. These steps should lay the groundwork; it will be up to the next pastor, and his staff, whether they wish to continue in this direction.

Base churches offer a lot of promise for the Catholic Church in the years ahead. Helping to address the priest shortage mentioned in the story above is just one obvious example. We just have to be sure we don't let the idea overwhelm us so we feel defeated before we start. Outline the various steps needed to restructure your parish, and then specify what action this step would mean for you and/or your ministry. Spell out at least five steps.

What About the Children?

The family as a unit is the core of the future! How does the restructuring of the parish into Small Church Communities influence our children? Unless they are formed deeply by these base churches, the considerable effort of this parish plan is not worth it at all. The children will be the church—and the world—in only a few years.

Although children and teenagers do not come to regular

meetings of SCCs except for special social times, the message is clear to these young people. Children see parents regularly giving up time on a free evening to meet with people from church—and enjoying these people! Children eventually ask about their parents' small groups—Why? What happens there? Isn't praying boring?

Children of parents involved in small churches come to see church as more than just an hour a week, more than just a small compartment of a larger life. More importantly, parents change in many ways because of their small group membership; in their values, life-styles, prayer habits. And the kids see these changes.

The following testimony comes from Paul, a father who sells computers to businesses. He persistently avoided joining a Small Church Community for six years and was never otherwise very involved in the parish. This is his story after two years:

A STORY

My SCC has encouraged some gradual changes in my life. It's changed who my best friends are. My best friends used to be a nice couple in my neighborhood who own two $20,000 cars and three or four mink and fox coats. Dad works 14 hours a day, six days a week, and Mom works 10 hours. The four children—ages two to eight—have a housekeeper and are neatly tucked into bed before their parents arrive home.

My new best friends in the SCC are ordinary Christians who work hard for a living and try to live their lives according to Christ's teachings. They commit time to their families and friends. My point is not to criticize my old best friends because they still are my friends, and I like them, but my goals and aspirations are very different from theirs. My SCC now influences my goals. Our children grow up so fast, they need our time, energy and, most of all, our love every day. We can't give them love if we're not with them, and we certainly can't buy it for them.

The slow change in my goals has also changed my children's goals; they no longer seem as interested in having designer shoes and clothes. They have chosen friends with similar interests and care for other people.

My SCC has changed my life, and my family's. Couples in small groups report that family life is visibly different, with better attitudes toward each other, greater ability to listen, changes in family priorities. Parents also begin, subtly and overtly, to communicate different perceptions about the church itself, about religious education and prayer in the home, about some kind of faith-sharing at home.

So many influences on today's children are beyond parents' control. Creating an alternative environment in the home is difficult—and even more complicated in a single parent home. Parish family life programs help for a time, but family challenges change daily as children mature. We found that SCCs are generally more effective for family life than parish family life programs because small communities reach more of the parish's population and are ongoing and reinforcing. The church just by being itself better at this basic level ends up giving Christian families—and their children— the help they deserve.

The contact between adults and children and among children of various families within a small church occurs to varying degrees. Families notice each other at Mass and linger afterwards. And meetings do take place in homes. Sometimes an SCC and its children take on a service project together. Often there is a social or two over the year. Some adults develop friendships and a social life through the SCC; others keep only to the meetings twice a month. In all cases, however, over a few years—usually sooner—children are influenced.

A STORY

Hello. I am a Catholic 14-year-old who goes to a public school. I listen to new-wave music and dress in the latest clothes. My parents belong to an SCC, St. Elizabeth Seton. They meet twice a month on Tuesdays or Thursdays. The people in the group mean a lot to my parents and me.

I know that it sounds really strange that some 14-year-old could be saying this but, believe it or not, it's true. I babysit for some of the couples in the group. Their children are special to me, and so are the parents. I can talk to adults in our church and I never could before. I never knew any adults before, and I wasn't very interested in changing that. But now that has changed. If I were having some sort of problem with my family, I could probably turn to one of these adults for help.

Recently our family went on vacation with others from the SCC and stayed at a home owned by one of the families in our group. No one could take showers or get much privacy; we were all together in one house. I had serious doubts about the whole thing.

On the way there I was going crazy with the thought of being with a bunch of kids I babysit for, and no shower for the whole weekend. I really thought I was going to die. After the state of shock of being there, I realized it wasn't going to be quite as bad as I had thought originally. All the kids and a couple of adults went to the sand dunes for the day. It was lots of fun.

I even got to talk to one of the adults. I told her how I had lightened my hair color and how my father got a little upset about it. She explained to me how my dad loved me so much that he didn't want me to grow up. Well, I had this bottle of Sun-In which I had no use for now, so I gave it to her.

On Sunday we all went to church together and then out to breakfast together. There was one strange thing I noticed: no one was sitting with his or her own family. My brother was sitting with a boy he never was friends with before. I was sitting at one table and my parents at another. I guess, in a way, we all became one big family within the church.

I learned a lot since that weekend. I learned the church can be fun—without praying all the time. And there's another thing I'm sure of. I sure am glad my parents joined an SCC.

Where Do We Go From Here?

We are all called to be church. Structuring all the parish activities to allow ordinary people to help each other connect everyday life and faith and structuring the parish into small permanent communities are viable ways to be the church in our time and in our culture.

Bringing people together to be church for each other—this is the pastoral role. So if you are a pastoral minister, or if you can influence one, I hope this book has provided you with a vision that inspires, as well as with practical steps for actually proceeding. If restructuring the parish does not seem the right direction for you, then what better plan can you come up with that:

- doesn't burn out pastoral staff
- is based on the reality of being the church
- connects everyday lived life with God
- has the same potential for deeply affecting the life of your parish?

How to Begin

Here, in summary form, are some basic steps for proceeding:

- Start with yourself by developing a reflective life-style.
- Share this vision with the pastor or a staff person or

with a few parishioners who can influence thinking in the parish.

- Begin one—or several—groups with some of these parish leaders and go through the initial experience, the second stage and so on.
- Begin to use each existing parish program as a means for people to help each other connect everyday life and faith.
- Keep looking out for prospective pastoral facilitators and praying for them.

And above all else, let us all keep praying for the church and for this work.

The National Alliance of Parishes Restructuring Into Communities (NAPRC) is available for two- to three-day workshops for the priests and key staff people of five or more parishes. You can contact NAPRC at 1000 Michigan Ave., Marysville, MI 48040-1466, 810-364-3500.

Bibliography

A bibliography for the process of structuring a parish where the ordinary parishioners help each other connect everyday life and faith regularly.

RESOURCES FOR THE VISION OF RESTRUCTURING THE PARISH

Creating Small Church Communities: A Plan for Restructuring the Parish and Renewing Catholic Life. $7.95. Available also in Spanish. St. Anthony Messenger Press, 1615 Republic Street, Cincinnati, OH 45210. (800) 488-0488.

20/20 Vision For the Parish, A Clear Direction for the Future. A 35-minute video featuring parishes, pastors and parishioners who speak to the whys and hows of restructuring parish from their own experience. Includes a 4+ hour study guide. $24.95 plus $3.00 postage. National Alliance for Parishes Restructuring Into Communities, 1000 Michigan Ave., Marysville, MI 48040-1466. (810) 364-3500.

Membership in the National Alliance (includes quarterly newsletter), address above.

Creating Small Faith Communities Video, a 90-minute video. Lecture style, with discussion questions. Useful for parish leadership. This is an in-depth presentation about restructuring parishes. $19.95. St. Anthony Messenger Press.

A six-session program (title to be announced) with interactive format and questions for the SCC to study the vision of restructuring the parish and how their own SCC fits into the total parish vision. Contact the National Alliance of

Parishes Restructuring Into Communities.

RESOURCES FOR PHASE ONE, A SMALL GROUP: THE BEGINNING
EXPERIENCE

Come As You Are, A Small Group Program about Everyday Living.
This is a 12-session program with a participant book for
each member of the group, a facilitator's book and audio
tapes. It is meant for a group that is beginning or a group
of people who may be experienced in small groups but
have never been together with each other in this particular
group. Available also in Spanish. Participant's journal
$4.95, Facilitator's book $14.95, 2 audiocassettes $11.95;
7 percent shipping and handling. The National Alliance of
Parishes Restructuring Into Communities.

RESOURCES FOR PHASE TWO, A SMALL COMMUNITY

*Praying Alone and Together: An 11-Session Prayer Module for Small
Communities* after the Phase One experience. Available also
in Spanish. $6.95. St. Anthony Messenger Press.

*Challenge 2000, A Daily Meditation Program based on The Spiritual
Exercises of St. Ignatius.* Good daily life and faith reflection
questions but weaker on the format for the group meeting.
$8.95. Tabor Publishing, 200 East Bethany Drive, Allen, TX
75002-3804. (214) 390-6300.

RESOURCES FOR PHASE THREE, THE SMALL CHURCH COMMUNITY

*Faith Sharing for Small Church Communities: Questions and
Commentaries on the Sunday Readings,* composed by 7,500
people in Small Church Communities from six continents,
with suggestions for the format of the meeting. Cycles A,
B and C in one book. Available also in Spanish. $9.95. St.
Anthony Messenger Press.

Quest, an attractive participant booklet with commentaries and
questions based on the Sunday readings, suggestions for
individual action response after the meeting and a clear

format for the meeting itself. Published three times a year. The Pastoral Department for Small Christian Communities, Archdiocese of Hartford, 467 Bloomfield Ave., Bloomfield, CT 06002. (203) 243-9642.

Vision 2000 (Cycle A), *Mission 2000* (Cycle B), *Action 2000* (Cycle C), by Mark Link. A pocket-sized book for each cycle, including a Scripture verse, a reflective piece and a simple question about one's own life and attitude. Excellent personal reflection but only a bare-bones group format. $8.95. Tabor Publishing, 200 East Bethany Drive, Allen, TX 75002-3804. (214) 390-6300.

OTHER HELPFUL RESOURCES FOR FOCUS QUESTIONS ON THE LECTIONARY

Breaking Open the Word of God, by Karen Hinman Powell and Joseph P. Sinwell. A different book for each of the three cycles of the lectionary for use in the RCIA. Paulist Press, 997 MacArthur Blvd., Mahwah, NJ 07430. (201) 825-7300.

Any of the other excellent materials for faith/life reflection on the Sunday Scriptures for use in the RCIA.

Serendipity Bible, by Lyman Coleman and others. $19.95. Serendipity House, Box 1012, Littleton, CO 80160. (800) 525-9563.

RESOURCE FOR THE FORMATION OF PASTORAL FACILITATORS FOR SCCS:

Pastoring the 'Pastors': Resources for Training and Supporting Pastoral Facilitators. Contains six initial formation sessions, three formats for annual retreats and material for the monthly meeting for Pastoral Facilitators. Available also in Spanish. $6.95. St. Anthony Messenger Press.

SCC RESOURCES FOR PARTICULAR SITUATIONS

For combining two smaller groupings or for bringing in a new person into an existing SCC:

— A program of six sessions soon to be available from the National Alliance of Parishes Restructuring Into Communities.

For the SCC (in Phase Three) to appreciate how it fits together with the other parish SCCs in the total vision of restructuring:

—A program of six sessions with interactive questions built around the study of the book *Creating Small Church Communities*. Available soon from the National Alliance of Parishes Restructuring Into Communities.

RESOURCES IN SPANISH

Acerca De La Vida Diaria y Lo Que Cuenta. May be *Ven Como Eres* (Un Programa Para Pequenas Grupos). National Alliance of Parishes Restructuring Into Communities.

Creando Pequenas Comunidades de Fe: Un Plan Para Reestructurar la Parroquia y Renovar la Vida Catolica (Edicion Revisada). St. Anthony Messenger Press.

Orando Solos y Juntos: Un Modulo de Oracion de 11 Sesiones Para las Pequenas Comunidades de Fe. St. Anthony Messenger Press.

Pastoreando a los Pastores: Recursos Para Entrenar y Apoyar a los Facilitadores Pastorales de Pequenas Comunidades de Fe. St. Anthony Messenger Press.

A p p e n d i x   B

Basic Principles for a Small-Group Agreement or Contract

1. *Don't miss, except for emergencies.* A group works because members make the group a priority.
2. *Share yourself.* Let people know you to the extent you are willing. How you feel and how you look at life matters.
3. *Listen closely to others.* Don't give advice, counsel or therapy (unless asked specifically), but let people know you understand and are trying to appreciate the feeling they are expressing.
4. *Never argue your point or badger another.* Be yourself, be firm, but don't try to win others over to your viewpoint. People can be different. In fact, differences enhance a group.
5. *Try to show support to each person in the group.* Help people see their strengths and confront them when they are not using their strengths.
6. *Expressing negative feelings can be helpful.* Bottled-up feelings can set up unspoken barriers. Avoid ridicule or attack. Focus on how someone's behavior in the group affects you and how the situation can be improved. A one-to-one talk can help sometimes.
7. *Don't talk about people behind their backs.*
8. *Nothing said leaves the group.*
9. *Take responsibility for the life of the community.* Take a turn facilitating or hosting the meeting. Do something that might help another's contribution to the group get noticed. Call an absent member. Pray for each other.

A p p e n d i x C

Sample Evaluations

FOR A SMALL CHURCH COMMUNITY:

What would deepen and improve our listening to each other? To our lives? To God?

How do we handle disagreements and conflict in this group?

Does our SCC see itself as church? How do we fit into the total vision of the parish? How can we grow in our sense of belonging to the larger church? Be specific.

How is this SCC meeting helping each of us be different in our family, work place, society, attitude toward the poor of the world? Be specific.

Do we often get bogged down in small talk? In discussion from the head instead of speaking and listening to life experience? What specific ways can we agree to that would deepen our time together?

Is our SCC depending too much on one or a few people? What are the ways that each person in our SCC is taking responsibility for the group?

What is the best thing we have going for us? What is the main obstacle to growth?

A p p e n d i x   D

Review of Life

PRAYER/REFLECTION

1. Have I been able to find time each day for some prayer and reflection? If not, what are the barriers?
2. Name an experience of the Lord—or of his absence—in these last two weeks. What did I hear?
3. What do I need most to persevere?

ACTION/REIGN OF GOD

4. What challenges am I experiencing in carrying my prayer/reflection into my family, work, society?
5. How is my attitude changing toward the most forgotten people in our society? What am I doing about them?

CHURCH

6. In what ways am I growing closer to the church, the Body of Christ?

RESOLUTION

7. For the next two weeks, what will be my one, clear-cut and simple plan or resolve? Whom will I ask to pray for me in this regard?

Stages of Group Development (Psychological)

	Beginning, Including	Control ("Kill the King")	Conflict
ISSUE TO BE FACED	Will I look foolish? Be accepted? Can I be myself?	Competition. Who sets the tone of the group? Who is important?	Answer person. Advice-giver. Trying to "convert" the other.
HELPFUL RESPONSE:	Clarity on expectations. Use experience questions. Teach each other listening skills.	Share responsibility for leading. Group evaluation for group. Notice each person's contribution.	Evaluate what's happening. Speak to the issue of conflict and deal with it.

Belonging (Sharing of Life/ Faith)	Intimacy (Followed by Withdrawal)	Termination
Trust.	Testing. Closeness, then second thoughts.	Issue of ending. The group dies.
Small groups of three. Quiet time. Hospitality.	Discuss stages of group development, including this one.	Face it. Ritualize.

These stages are a normal part of growth. A particular stage cannot be skipped. The group can always regress to an earlier stage. A mature group should look at this progression as time goes on, but not become analytical about itself.

Other *Called to Be Church* titles:

- *Faith Sharing for Small Church Communities: Questions and Commentaries on the Sunday Readings* B1663

- *Pastoring the 'Pastors': Resources for Training and Supporting Pastoral Facilitators* B5979

- *Praying Alone and Together: An 11-Week Prayer Module for Small Faith Communities* B8978